ALSO BY JAMES EMERY

Life-Defining Moments

Long Night's Journey into Day

Rethinking the Church

A Search for the Spiritual

You Can Experience a Spiritual Life

You Can Experience—a Purposeful Life

You Can Experience—an Authentic Life

Merry Christmas From
Mecklenburg Community
Church
www.mecklenburg.org

Wrestling with God

Loving the God We Don't Understand

James Emery White

IVP Books

An imprint of InterVarsity Press
Downers Grove, Illinois

InterVarsity Press
P.O. Box 1400, Downers Grove, IL 60515-1426
World Wide Web: www.ivpress.com
E-mail: email@ivpress.com

First published as Embracing the Mysterious God.

InterVarsity Press® *is the book-publishing division of InterVarsity Christian Fellowship/USA*®*, a student movement active on campus at hundreds of universities, colleges and schools of nursing in the United States of America, and a member movement of the International Fellowship of Evangelical Students. For information about local and regional activities, write Public Relations Dept., InterVarsity Christian Fellowship/USA, 6400 Schroeder Rd., P.O. Box 7895, Madison, WI 53707-7895, or visit the IVCF website at <www.intervarsity.org>.*

All Scripture quotations, unless otherwise indicated, are taken from the Holy Bible, New International Version®. NIV®. *Copyright* ©*1973, 1978, 1984 by International Bible Society. Used by permission of Zondervan Publishing House. All rights reserved.*

Lyrics on p. 34 are from "Closer to Fine," words and music by Emily Sallers, ©*1989 EMI Virgin Songs, Inc., and Godhap Music. All rights controlled and administered by EMI Virgin Songs, Inc. All rights reserved. International copyright secured. Used by permission.*

The story in chapter three of a woman returning to church is retold by permission.

Every effort has been made to trace and contact copyright holders for additional materials quoted in this book. The author will be pleased to rectify any omissions in future editions if notified by the copyright holders.

Design: Cindy Kiple
Images: Nancy Simmerman/Getty Images

ISBN 978-0-8308-3363-4

Printed in the United States of America ∞

Library of Congress Cataloging-in-Publication Data

White, James Emery, 1961-
Wrestling with God: loving the God we don't understand / James
Emery White.—[Rev. ed.].
    p. cm.
Rev. ed.: Embracing the mysterious God. c2003.
Includes bibliographical references.
ISBN 978-0-8308-3363-4 (pbk.: alk. paper)
1. Spiritual life—Christianity. I. White, James Emery, 1961-
Embracing the mysterious God. II. Title.
BV4501.3.W464 2008
248.4—dc22
                                                                    2008008992

P   18   17   16   15   14   13   12   11   10   9   8   7   6   5   4   3   2   1
Y   23   22   21   20   19   18   17   16   15   14   13   12   11   10   09   08

CONTENTS

ACKNOWLEDGMENTS

I am deeply indebted in my life with Christ to InterVarsity Christian Fellowship, the parent ministry of my publisher. I gave my life to Christ's leadership after friends invited me to an InterVarsity meeting at the beginning of my sophomore year in college. I was discipled and then given my first opportunity to lead by InterVarsity staff. I felt God's call to vocational ministry confirmed through InterVarsity's 1981 Urbana conference in Illinois and 1982 National Leadership Institute at Bear Trap Ranch in Colorado.

During those years I read IVP books that deeply formed my life and thought—books such as Colin Brown's *Philosophy*, Os Guinness's *The Dust of Death*, Paul Little's *Know Why You Believe*, Richard Lovelace's *Dynamics of Spiritual Life*, Robert Boyd Munger's *My Heart—Christ's Home*, J. I. Packer's *Knowing God*, Becky Pippert's *Out of the Saltshaker*, Francis Schaeffer's *Escape from Reason*, James Sire's *The Universe Next Door*, John Stott's *Basic Christianity* and John White's *The*

Fight. Those books are still shaping me today.

I have no idea whether I am the only person won to Christ and then discipled through InterVarsity who has come full circle and ended up as one of their authors, but this project fulfills a long-held desire within my heart. Thanks, Cindy, for making it possible.

Acknowledgment must also go to my assistant, Glynn Goble, who serves my life with joy, enthusiasm and good humor. Mecklenburg Community Church continues to find it within its heart to support my life and ministry, and for that I remain grateful.

As always, the greatest acknowledgment goes to my wife, Susan, who makes every page possible.

James Emery White
Charlotte, North Carolina

INTRODUCTION
Loving the God We Don't Understand

Coming to faith is like falling in love.

For some it is head-over-heels love at first sight, with a rush to the altar. Others find the entire idea of spiritual things wholly to their unliking, only to discover that many of their first impressions were mistaken. A begrudging acceptance moves toward appreciation and then, almost unnoticed, slips over the line into heartfelt embrace. Yet in either case Malcolm Muggeridge was right in observing that in the end, coming to faith remains for all a "sense of homecoming, of picking up the threads of a lost life, of responding to a bell that had long been ringing, of taking a place at a table that had long been vacant."[1]

But then romance crashes headlong into reality. We give ourselves to God, and then struggle profoundly with the relationship. We are drawn inexorably in, and then find ourselves wanting to flee in fear. We move from faith to doubt, trust to confusion, intimacy to a feeling of abandonment. We find that living with God is not easy.

Most respond to the struggle with guilt, presuming that faith should somehow be free of complexity and challenge. They blame themselves, lamenting the condition of their soul that would allow such thoughts and feelings toward God. Their struggle is not embraced but confessed.

Others simply dismiss the entire affair, choosing to live on the surface of faith, condemning their spiritual lives to a bloodless existence that brings neither life nor death. Their lack of spiritual concern leads them to neither deny or embrace the struggle. Then, in a terrible moment when vibrant faith is required, they experience the anguish of an untested soul.

Some respond to the struggle with resentment. They separate themselves from God and all things pertaining to him. As C. S. Lewis once remarked, they place God in the dock where—judged by their expectations of how life should be—God cannot escape indictment.

Yet guilt, neglect and resentment are not the goals of God's relation to us. This God has not only made himself known to us but has fallen madly in love with us. Our Creator has pursued his creation throughout time—even to the point of dying on our behalf. He speaks of us as bride and himself as Bridegroom. This God longs for the deepest of intimacies.

He seeks our love—heart, soul, mind and strength—a love with such force that it cannot help but overflow to those around us. Jesus' words along these lines have become known as the Great Commandment—in truth, the portrait of a Lover's dream.

But this only adds to our dilemma.

To return such love in such a manner involves total devotion, the very thing our struggle keeps us from giving. To speak of heart, soul, mind and strength is to speak of the totality of life itself. As Abraham Kuyper, founder of the Free University of Amsterdam, once declared, "There is not a single inch of any sphere of my life to which Christ does not say, '*mine!*' "

We tend to remove ourselves from the staggering ramifications of this by intellectualizing the affair. Rather than responding to God in like manner—relationally—we engage his proposal philosophically, as an abstract idea to be evaluated on its virtuous intent.

This was the response of the person who first prompted Jesus to speak along these lines:

> A wonderful answer, Teacher! So lucid and accurate—that God is one and there is no other. And loving him with all passion and intelligence and energy, and loving others as well as you love yourself. Why, that's better than all offerings and sacrifices put together!

But intellectual affirmation was not what Jesus was after.

Thus he replied, "You're almost there, right on the border of God's kingdom" (Mark 12:32-34 The Message).

Jesus understood that *knowing* you should love God with all of your being was distinct from embracing that kind of love *experientially*. Which means the struggle cannot be avoided.

Guilt, apathy and resentment will keep our souls from responding to the call of our creation. The struggle to live in relationship with our loving God has marked the lives of all the great souls, from the Desert Fathers to the medieval mystics, from the ancient martyrs to the modern saints.

And it must mark our own.

If the tension points in our relationship with God cannot be owned, talked about and laid bare before him, then not only will we be unable to receive the love for which we were created, we will be unable to return it. We hunger not merely for encounter with God but for authenticity with God. We want to know and be known in order to throw ourselves fully into the wonder and tumult of his mystery.

But this relationship demands more than acquiescence; it demands transparency and deep knowledge. A knowing kind of love demands that we explore what we often do not wish to explore, namely, the complexities of our relationship with God: the complexities that strike at the heart of the relationship and threaten its very existence. Any attempt to approach God independent of this strikes me as false.

I have always resonated with C. S. Lewis, "the most dejected and reluctant convert in all England."[2] Because his journey took him through paralyzing issues that often beset the embrace of faith, he was able to speak about matters of faith with more clarity than virtually anyone else in modern Christendom.

But such a journey is rare. When conflicts arise, we bury them, turn a cold shoulder, explode in emotion or simply run away. We think that such pseudo-community is the easiest and best way to live.

It's not.

Until we are willing to explore the dynamics that exist between us at the deepest relational levels, we will never draw near and experience community. M. Scott Peck speaks of this as entering into chaos, for it is messy, frightening and difficult.[3] And he's right. I cannot begin to tell you how gut-wrenching conflict resolution and truth-telling in human relationships is for me, but I have found them to be even more daunting tasks to pursue with God. There are questions reverberating through my mind I do not want to speak; feelings I do not want to own; doubts I do not want to surface—particularly as I know that they reveal far more about me than him.

Yet only when my struggle is embraced can I journey toward that which I long for: intimacy with God.

And that is the one journey that is worth everything.

PART ONE

The Struggle
of Our Hearts

The heart is an amazing organ. As a working muscle, over the course of an average lifetime it will beat, or more accurately *pump*, over 2.5 billion times, usually without maintenance, and without replacement.

And it's strong. Though only about 10.5 ounces in weight, the human heart operates with the equivalent energy of a one-horsepower engine, moving two thousand gallons of blood each day. Its valves alone operate four to five thousand times per hour.[1]

But that's nothing compared to what's inside of it: *Courage. Valor. Strength. Endurance. Passion.*

The ancient Hebrews saw the heart as the seat of the will, the command center of all emotions and the domain of all desires. Decisions were made, and direction taken, as a function of the heart. Commitment was birthed and, if nurtured, took root.

Jesus said "Blessed are the pure in heart" (Matthew 5:8) because purity is housed in the heart. Conversely, his greatest accusation was "These people honor me with their lips, / but their hearts are far from me" (Matthew 15:8), for it is within our hearts that we choose for or against God. The heart is the place from which we return the passionate love God has shown to us. It is where we, as the beloved, respond to the One who first loved us.

And many have chosen to respond. You see it in King David's wild dancing in front of the Ark of the Covenant, or in Mary as a teenage virgin accepting a very unplanned pregnancy. You see it in the medieval writings of Julian of Norwich or the Renaissance words of Teresa of Ávila, who told of their love for God with the unabashed language of adolescent romance. You see it in the life of Brother Lawrence, a seventeenth-century monk who wrote that he couldn't even turn over an omelet in his pan without thinking of his affection for God. You see it in the acts of Mother Teresa, who when asked how she could reach out to the poor and destitute in the slums of Calcutta, simply said that in their faces she saw Jesus in a distressing disguise.

Such hearts for God are easily seen but less easily cultivated. We are by nature skeptical that anyone is worthy of such devotion. To give our hearts is to make ourselves vulnerable—able to be wounded—and our hearts have too often been torn asunder. Bringing our emotions to God is a difficult journey, made more difficult when we reflect on the most troubling thought of all: our hearts may not be safe from his.

One

THE BETRAYAL OF GOD

Be merciful to me, LORD, for I am faint;
O LORD, heal me, for my bones are in agony.
My soul is in anguish.
How long, O LORD, how long?
PSALM 6:2-3

F ew relationships with God are free of fist-shaking, epithet-hurling moments. We become overwhelmed with the idea that God should have prevented something or intervened in some way to alter the course of events that have marred our life. At the very least he should have come to our rescue once the pain, suffering, illness, tragedy or attack began. We feel nothing less than betrayed.

Such matters are deeply personal, an affair of the heart. Like a jilted lover, we feel our faith shaken to its foundation when the Divine Lover acts in a way we don't expect. As Bono of the musical group U2, himself a person of struggling faith, has mused, "How do you explain a love and logic at the heart of the universe when the world is so out of whack?"[1]

In the 2001 season finale of NBC's *The West Wing*, President Josiah Bartlet, a person of faith, wrestles with the death of his secretary in a drunk-driving accident and the impending revelation of his own multiple sclerosis. His anguish over life's cruel twists leads him to linger in the National Cathedral after his secretary's funeral, offering his heart to God.

But his prayer doesn't begin with "Our Father, who art in heaven, hallowed be thy name." Instead, with nerves raw and faith tested, the president curses God, calling him a "feckless thug."

That was just what was offered in English. The rest of the prayer, perhaps to avoid a rush on the network's switchboard, was offered in Latin. Here's the translation:

> Am I really to believe that these are the acts of a loving God? A just God? A wise God? To h——with your punishments. I was your servant here on earth. And I spread your word and I did your work. To h—— with your punishments. To h—— with you.

The scene ends with Bartlet, in a gesture of contempt, crushing a cigarette butt on the sacred ground of the cathedral floor.[2]

When we wrestle with God's apparent betrayal, we still cling tenuously to our faith, like desperate men and women who feel they have no other choice. But what kind of faith, and what kind of relationship with this God who still calls for our heart? As a Sunday school member remarked toward God regarding the death of a friend's child, "If You took my son, I wouldn't doubt You were alive; I just wouldn't talk with You anymore."[3]

The problem of evil and suffering, from a theological perspective, is famously presented in three statements:

1. Evil and suffering exist.
2. A good God would not want evil and suffering, and an all-powerful God would not tolerate it.
3. Therefore God is either far from good, or far from all-powerful.

Neither of these conclusions fits the God of the Bible. Theologians attempt to answer this conundrum by constructing theodicies —philosophical and theological arguments that defend God's power and goodness. For most people, however, even the best theodicies are unsatisfying. While cerebral and often correct, when set before the journey of the heart they come across as heart*less*. We don't want an intellectual discourse; we want to know why God didn't keep us from being hurt. We want to be assured that we are still loved by God and that it is safe for us to return that love. It is not the mind that cries out, but the emotions.

"Not that I am (I think) in much danger of ceasing to believe in God. The real danger is of coming to believe such dreadful things about Him. The conclusion I dread is not 'So there's no God after all,' but 'So this is what God's really like. Deceive yourself no longer.' "

C. S. LEWIS, *A GRIEF OBSERVED*

We need a story larger than the story of our pain, one

that allows our hearts to remain tender and surrendered. Sadly, few Christians know this larger story—a story that places God in the midst of our suffering so that love would win the day.

To tell such a story, one must begin at the very beginning.

IN THE BEGINNING

God made us in order to love us. We were tenderly crafted and designed, each as an individual, for the purpose of being known and deeply cherished. Yet this means that we were also given the freedom to make choices with our lives, to live as fully conscious, self-determining beings.

Even to the point of determining ourselves whether we respond to the Creator's love.

God did not choose to seduce us against our will. Instead, he determined to woo us, knowing that we might very well spurn his love. But this was the only way to have relationship *be* relationship. Danish philosopher Søren Kierkegaard writes of the risk and complexity of this divine desire through the tale of a king:

> Suppose there was a king who loved a humble maiden.
> . . . Every statesman feared his wrath and dared not breathe a word of displeasure; every foreign state trembled before his power and dared not omit sending ambassadors with congratulations for the nuptials. . . .
> Then there awoke in the heart of the king an anxious thought. . . . Would she be happy in the life at his side?

22

Would she be able to summon confidence enough never to remember . . . that he was a king and she had been a humble maiden? For if this memory were to waken in her soul, and like a favored lover sometimes steal her thoughts away from the king, luring her reflections into the seclusion of a silent grief; or if this memory sometimes passed through her soul like the shadow of death over the grave: where would then be the glory of their love?[4]

The king wanted true love, but how could he assure that her love for him would be true?

He could bring her to the palace, covering her with silk and jewels in an effort to coax her affection. But this would be a purchased heart.

He could come to her cottage, casting a shadow of glory and power over its humble surroundings, driving her to her knees in awe and wonder. But that would be an overpowered heart.

No, neither elevation of her or himself would achieve the desired end—only his own descent. The king became a humble servant and sought to win her heart.

This is the dynamic at the heart of human existence. God could have *bought* our love or *overpowered* our will, but his relationship with us would have been left meaningless. God wanted our relationships, with him and with others, to be real. So he took the risk of creating us free.

Adam and Eve were the first to experience this freedom. A

tree of forbidden fruit in the middle of the Garden of Eden stood as the great authenticator that the love between the first humans and God was real. Then they chose to eat the fruit—consciously, purposefully deciding to violate the boundaries of the relationship. The Lover was spurned.

And then all hell broke loose.

Not the Way It's Supposed to Be

The decision of the first humans to reject their relationship with God radically altered his original design for how the world would operate and how life would be lived. They had forever stained the relationship that had been intended for eternity within the Lover's heart. Theologians have termed this the Fall, and they suggest that we now live in a "fallen" world. When Satan told Eve that if she ate of the tree's fruit she would not die, he lied. That day, death was born to the human race.

Few of us find it easy to believe that the human race continues to inherit the consequences of one act of disobedience. Yet reflecting on his experience in a Japanese internment camp during World War II, Langdon Gilkey notes that a pervasive warping of our wills is the most accurate description of the reality of life. In that camp, prisoners representing a cross-section of humanity were forced to participate in a living laboratory of community. "What the doctrine of sin has said about man's present state," Gilkey concluded, "seemed to fit the facts as I found them."[5]

In the movie *Grand Canyon*, an attorney tries to get around a traffic jam but gets lost as a series of wrong turns takes him into a part of town that is the furthest thing from the tony suburbs of his world. His expensive car stalls, and he uses his cell phone to call for a tow truck. As he waits, five young street toughs circle his car and begin to threaten him. The tow truck arrives and the driver begins to hook up the car, ignoring the five young men trying to steal it. They then turn their attention toward him.

The driver of the tow truck takes the leader of the group aside and says, "Man, the world ain't supposed to work like this. Maybe you don't know that, but this ain't the way it's supposed to be. I'm supposed to be able to do my job without askin' you if I can. And that dude is supposed to be able to wait with his car without you rippin' him off. Everything's supposed to be different than what it is here."[6]

The results of our collective choice to turn away from God result in not just moral sin but natural evil as well. "The whole creation has been groaning" (Romans 8:22), which is why we have earthquakes and tidal waves, volcanoes and mudslides, wildfires and birth defects, famine and AIDS. Our world is "the stained planet," according to Philip Yancey, a cosmic "scream . . . that something is wrong, . . . that the entire human condition is out of whack."[7]

These are far from original insights; the medieval Christian philosopher Boethius aptly noted that "evil is not so much an infliction as a deep set infection."[8] This raises a provocative point: God is not behind what is tragic with this world, much less responsible for it. People are.

Our hearts shy away from God in light of our pain and the pain of the world around us. We feel betrayed, yet we fail to see that it is we who have done the betraying.

Philip Yancey, a writer who has invested much of his life exploring these issues, was contacted by a television producer after the death of Princess Diana to explain how God could have possibly allowed such a tragic accident. "Could it have had something to do with a drunk driver going ninety miles an hour in a narrow tunnel?" he asked the producer. "How, exactly, was God involved?"

When boxer Ray "Boom Boom" Mancini killed a Korean boxer in a match, he said in a press conference, "Sometimes I wonder why God does the things he does."

In a letter to a Christian family therapist, a teenage girl asked why God would allow her to get pregnant.

In her official confession, South Carolina mother Susan Smith said that as she pushed the car holding her two sons into a lake, she ran after the car screaming, "Oh God! Oh God, no! . . . Why did you let this happen?"[9]

Yancey raises the decisive question: What exactly was the role God played in a boxer pummeling his opponent, a teenager abandoning her virtue, or a mother drowning her children? God has let us choose, and our choices have brought continual pain and heartache and destruction. Our self-destructive bent seemingly knows no bounds.

A FATHER'S LOVE

Some may say, "Well, if God knew how things would turn out, he should have never created us!" because everything from cancer to concentration camps just isn't worth it. Yet when we blithely say such things, we betray how little we know of true love. Yes, the freedom to choose that God gave each of us has resulted in heartache and even tragedy. It is tempting to say that everyone—including God—would have been better off never having to endure it. But that's not the way love—real love, at least—works.

To remember this, I need only reflect on one of the most defining realities of my life: my own role as a father. As I write these words, my oldest daughter is beginning her freshman year in high school. And because of this fact, all summer I've been a wreck.

I thought sending her to her first birthday party was hard. She came home in tears because the birthday girl announced at the start of a game that "everyone can play but Rebecca."

I thought leaving her at school for an entire day for the first time was hard. And then I learned that another child had purposefully tripped her on the playground.

I thought that pulling out splinters, or holding her through the night when she had a fever, was hard.

I thought that watching her experience the onset of puberty, and the painful awkwardness and insecurity of becoming a teenager, was hard.

Now send your first child to high school, where she can

wound and be wounded in ways that were unthinkable the day you first held her in your arms. Then you'll know hard.

But let me—the one who loves her more than anyone, the one who would lay down his life for her in an instant—tell you what has *never* entered my mind:

Never having her.

Never bringing her into the world.

Never going through life with her.

Even though she can reject me and tear out my heart by hurting herself as well as others, if someone were to say, "Why do you even bother?" my only reply would be, "Because she is my daughter." And having known fathers who have endured far more anguish than I have, suffering through prodigal years, chronic illnesses and even untimely death, I can say confidently that no matter the cost, the value of bringing our children into the world goes without question.

Suffering, Christian faith tells us, cannot be dismissed as mere injustice or punishment for our sins. Suffering is "a harrowing invitation to a higher dialogue": love.[10] Without the willingness to be wounded on the deepest of levels, we cannot have authentic relationships on the deepest of levels. And this is God's great longing: to commune with us for eternity.

So Where Is God?

So where am I in the potential pain of my daughter's life—the pain that might come her way, and that might flow back to me because I chose to have her? Right by her side, caring, weeping and longing to hold her in my arms—the same place God is with my pain, and your pain, and all of the pain in this world.

God is longing to hold each of us. The Bible says that God is "close to the brokenhearted. . . . / The righteous face many troubles / but the LORD rescues them from each and every one" (Psalm 34:18-19 NLT). And those who have opened up their hearts to God's presence and comfort in the midst of their pain have found this to be true.

But that's not all that God has done. He heals the wounds that come from our choices by entering into the suffering process *with us* in order to lift us *out* of it. God himself came to earth in the person of Jesus and *suffered*. He *knows* about pain. He *knows* about rejection. He *knows* about hunger, injustice, and cruelty because he has *experienced* it firsthand.

An ancient graffito on the Palatine in Rome shows a crucified figure with a donkey's head, bearing the inscription "Alexamenos worships his god." Though meant to disparage and even mock, the image rings true. We worship, as German theologian Jürgen Moltmann observed, the *crucified* God. Jesus on the cross was God entering into the reality of human suffering, experiencing it just as we do in order to demonstrate that even when we use our free will to reject him, his love never ends. He suffered so that we might use our free will and choose again, this time making the *right* choice.

Frederick Buechner put it this way: "Like a father saying about his sick child, 'I'd do anything to make you well,' God finally calls his own bluff and does it."[11] The ultimate healing has come. Our greatest and most terrible affliction has been addressed. God has given us the greatest answer to our questions: himself.

So the real question is whether we will allow the reality of pain and suffering in this world to drive us *away* from God or simply walk toward him in the darkness, knowing that the Light exists. The most basic principle in our struggles, writes Os Guinness, is that "we do not know why, but we know why we trust God who knows why." And so we pray a simple but profound prayer: "Father, I do not understand you, but I trust you."[12]

For his will be the final word, and it will be not only good, but best.

THE NOT YET

The song "40," based on the Fortieth Psalm, often marked the end of U2 concerts following the events of September 11, 2001. Tens of thousands of people nightly sang the refrain, "How long to sing this song?" Bono, lead singer of the group, reflected, "How long . . . hunger? How long . . . hatred? How long until creation grows up and the chaos of its precocious, hell-bent adolescence has been discarded? I thought it odd that the vocalizing of such questions could bring such comfort: to me too."[13]

But precisely those such questions bring comfort. Bold living in light of our fallenness and a frank embrace of the realities of a fallen world are the marks of faith. Faith embraces emotional anguish but contains emotions in the shadow of the character of God—or the knowledge of the story at hand. There is order in our apparent chaos; God exists, and his loving purposes can be trusted. A sense of betrayal comes from a sense of confusion, but the truth is that God loves us passionately and lives with more pain from that love than we could ever imagine.

This is the greater story—the one in which I must place my own.

Two

THE EXCLUSIVITY OF GOD

*If salvation lay ready to hand and could be discovered
without great labour, how could it be possible
that it should be neglected almost by everybody? But all noble
things are as difficult as they are rare.*
SPINOZA *ETHICS* 5.42

I couldn't resist. All I had to do was answer twenty questions
about my concept of God, the afterlife and human nature,
and "Belief-O-Matic" would tell me what religion—if any—I
practiced—or ought to be practicing.[1]

Tongue-in-cheek (I hope), it added the following warning:
"Belief-O-Matic assumes no legal liability for the ultimate
fate of your soul."

I took the test, answering questions about the number and
nature of deities I thought existed, the origins of the physical
universe and life on earth, what happens to humans after
death, the path to salvation and prayer. After logging my
twenty answers, I waited anxiously for my chosen faith.

I was 100 percent Eastern Orthodox, 100 percent Roman Catholic and 100 percent Conservative Christian/Protestant. So much for historic schisms and denominational divides. But that's OK—a friend of mine, also an evangelical Christian, took the same test and was told that he is equal parts Orthodox, Quaker and Sikh.

I always knew there was something funny about him.

Belief-O-Matic speaks volumes about one of the most deeply held convictions of our day. Faith has become private and, by extension, custom-designed—little more than a matter of personal preference. The very concept of religious reality is rejected outright. Radical subjectivity has become the spiritual *ideal*. As the Indigo Girls proclaimed in their song "Closer to Fine":

> There's more than one answer to these questions
> pointing me in a crooked line.
> The less I seek my source for some definitive,
> the closer I am to fine.

Such sentiments have led to the popular acceptance of the Zen proverb "If you meet the Buddha on the road, kill him": any idea of God that someone could articulate is too shallow to be real, and is thus false and even dangerous. The intriguing website <www.killingthebuddha.com> embraces this proverb and attempts to shape a faith for those who are convinced they can be little more than faithless.

Each of us wants there to be truth. We want clear direction

and, yes, a single way to live. Jesus gave us our wildest dream, and one of our deepest struggles, when he proclaimed, "I am the way and the truth and the life. No one comes to the Father except through me" (John 14:6). He didn't say that he was "a" way, "a" truth or "a" life but *the* way, *the* truth and *the* life. And unless we come to Christ as our Leader and Forgiver, we cannot be in a saving relationship with God.

This sense of exclusivity has marked the Christian faith from its inception. The exclusivism that surrounded the teachings of Jesus were scandalous. Cyprian's famous declaration *"Extra ecclesiam nulla salus"* ("There is no salvation outside the church") rang loudly from the early third century until the end of the Middle Ages. The Reformation concepts *sola fidei, sola scriptura*, and *sola gratia* (faith alone, Scripture alone, grace alone) were equally narrow understandings of how one gained acceptance by God. People the world over throughout Christian history have been scandalized by the exclusive claims of Christian faith.

And they still are.

On the most foundational emotional level, who wouldn't resent the implication that they are leading a life of spiritual futility simply because they don't embrace another person's beliefs (particularly when you believe that the beliefs *belong* to the person)? Even Christians are often confused about the eternal destiny of deeply moral and spiritual people who embrace a religion other than our own. The "rightness" of it seems jaded, and the idea of salvation in Christ alone outmoded. We begin to wonder if John Godfrey Saxe's famous poem "The Blind Men and the Elephant" might be true to spiritual things after all: are we all groping blindly in the dark, proclaiming one small part of the indescribable as the ultimate and final truth?

THE GOOD IN OTHER RELIGIONS

Walter Truett Anderson has observed that we live in an "age of over-exposure to otherness."[2] Religious groups, sects, cults, movements, philosophies and worldviews abound in incredible numbers and diversity. When it comes to an authoritative spiritual text, we can choose from the Bible, the Bhagavad-Gita, the Qur'an and the Book of Mormon. When it comes to religious leaders, we can follow the Pope, the Dalai Lama, Hare Krishna, Buddha or Muhammad. And when it comes to groups, we can align with Mormons, Jehovah's Witnesses, Wiccans, Muslims, Jews, Christians or Scientologists. And that's only the beginning. David Barrett, editor of the World Christian Encyclopedia, has identified 9,900 distinct religions in the world, with two or three new religions added every day.[3] The most recent edition of his encyclopedia lists over 33,000 denominations within Christianity alone.[4] We live in a culture that Malise Ruthven has aptly termed a "divine supermarket."[5]

Peter Berger has observed that religion no longer serves as a "sacred canopy" underneath which all of our life—socially and culturally—could receive ultimate meaning.[6] Instead, individuals express spiritual identity in one of thousands upon thousands of equally viable, culturally diverse "umbrellas," which causes us to struggle with the idea that a single world-view can provide the ultimate insight into the human condition. These other pathways can't *all* be wrong, can they?

In truth, Jesus does not force me to say that other religions and philosophies are all wrong, or that they offer no spiritual insight into the human condition. As C. S. Lewis once wrote, "If you are a Christian you do not have to believe that all the other religions are simply wrong all through. . . . If you are a Christian, you are free to think that all these religions, even the queerest ones, contain at least some hint of the truth."[7]

> *"All truth is God's truth."*
> CLEMENT STROMATA 1.94

If all truth is God's truth, then it remains true wherever I find it. As a Christian I can appreciate the truth in much of Buddhist thought, such as the first two of four Noble Truths: there is a lot of suffering in the world, and our desires are often at the root of such suffering. Buddhism also espouses much clearly moral teaching: you should not take life in any form; you should not steal or lie; you should not engage in immoral sexual behavior; you should not take anything intoxicating.

Yet there are significant tension points between Buddhism and Christian faith. The Dalai Lama himself has stated that the central doctrines of Buddhism and Christianity are incompatible. You cannot be, according to the Dalai Lama, a

Buddhist Christian or a Christian Buddhist.

Christianity professes a personal God; Buddhism does not acknowledge even a higher being. Christianity sees *what* we desire rather than desire itself as the root of much suffering. Further, Christianity attests that sin and failure in human life is met with grace and forgiveness from God. The ultimate goal of life—in the case of Christianity, eternity with God—is not something we must earn but something given freely by God to us when we ask it of him. For the Buddhist, the ultimate goal of life—a state of ultimate peace called nirvana—is reached only through personal effort. Sin cannot be forgiven; it must be personally compensated for.

The greatest distinction between Buddhism and Christianity, however, has to do with Jesus. Some Buddhists believe in *bodhisattvas,* people who have achieved enlightenment but refuse to enter nirvana in order to help others achieve enlightenment, but there is no sense of a savior sent by God for the sake of everyone in the world. In contrast, Jesus does not simply help people along the way but provides the way of salvation through the giving of his life for ours.

How can we account for the good in other religions? The Bible attests that "the heavens declare the glory of God" (Psalm 19:1); thus God has revealed himself generally to those who have had no contact with the special revelation found in Jesus and the Scriptures.

We can also acknowledge a sense of God's common grace. Though the details are often debated, Christians generally affirm that God extends a degree of favor to all people regardless of the state of their relationship with him. Richard Mouw notes that what is good and right and true in the world reflects God's common grace: "God takes delight in Benjamin Franklin's wit and in Tiger Woods's putts and in some well-crafted narrative paragraphs in a Salman Rushdie novel . . . even if those accomplishments are in fact achieved by non-Christian people."[8]

But God's common grace and general revelation are limited in scope, which is why religions such as Buddhism must ultimately be rejected. The heavens may declare a God, but what kind of God? Such particular knowledge can come only through special revelation, as is found in the Bible. And while God's common grace flows freely, any sort of "saving good" comes only through *regenerative grace*—the grace revealed through direct encounters with Christ. Though some deeds, thoughts and lifestyles are morally laudable, salvation cannot be achieved through them.[9]

Christians are not exclusivists so much as *particularists*, for we evaluate other religious traditions from a Christian perspective. God's self-revelation has broken into the world through a myriad of ways, both natural and unique, but what he has revealed about himself can be interpreted rightly only in light of his full revelation in Christ. God has always been in view, as John Calvin suggested, but our vision lacks focus and definition without the corrective lens of Jesus Christ.

INTOLERANCE

But isn't this intolerant? And if there is one thing we do not want to be, it is intolerant.

"Toleration is one of the most attractive and widespread ideals of our day," writes Alan Levine. "It is . . . the predominant ethos of all civilizations in the modern world."[10] The degree to which toleration has become ingrained within our culture was evidenced in Allan Bloom's observations of higher education. Students have been taught to fear not error but intolerance. "Relativism is necessary to open-ness; and this is the virtue, the only virtue, which all primary education for more than fifty years has dedicated itself to inculcating." The point is not to really *be* right by uncovering truth, but "not to think you are right at all."[11]

"There is one thing a professor can be absolutely certain of: almost every student entering the university believes, or says he believes, that truth is relative."

ALLAN BLOOM, THE
CLOSING OF
THE AMERICAN MIND

But should we elevate tolerance, without nuance, to such a lofty level? Even John Locke, one of the early modern theorists of toleration and the philosopher perhaps most associated with its doctrine, believed that there needed to be limits to the idea. Shouldn't the Christian? For tolerance is far from a "one size fits all" idea, and its application far from one-dimensional.[12]

The first application of tolerance is *legal*. Cries against the legislation of morality speak to this application. Of course, all laws involve the legislation of morality, but there should be great tolerance in the law for diverse viewpoints and beliefs. The alternative stifles the freedom of opinion or the freedom to worship as one chooses. And nothing in Christianity would advocate the refusal of legal tolerance. Indeed, the Bible is a great advocate of legal tolerance, providing the philosophical basis for much of democracy's contours of thought.

The second application of tolerance is *social*, or *cultural*. Social tolerance seeks to care about others and remain open to them relationally regardless of such things as their views, ethnicity or sex. The great ethic of the Bible and the life-model of Jesus espouse this form of tolerance without reservation. If Jesus stood for anything, it was open, loving acceptance of others as people who mattered to God. This was the basis for much of the great civil rights movement of the United States, as led by the Reverend Dr. Martin Luther King, Jr.

The third form of tolerance is *intellectual*—accepting what someone believes as right regardless of what you believe or think is right.[13] Only in this sense should Christianity be considered intolerant. Jesus did not believe that everything and everyone was right. The Bible holds that there is right and wrong, true and false, and it is wildly intolerant in saying so.

But so are we all.

APPROPRIATELY INTOLERANT

Suppose someone came up to me and said, "I believe that the best way to improve the performance of your car is to pour sand into the gas tank." I could easily be tolerant of that person legally, not to mention socially, without buying into his beliefs about my car's performance. People are welcome to believe whatever they want about automotive fuel, but I don't *have* to accept their beliefs as best. Simply put, I can hold to the value that other people have a right to their beliefs without believing that all points of view are equally valid.

Syndicated columnist Ellen Goodman has confessed that she is a begrudging skeptic of all ideas being more or less equal. "Sometimes, an open mind comes perilously close to being an empty mind. Sometimes, tolerance is a way to avoid wrestling for the truth. Pluralism is not always the acceptance of a range of hard-won views, but a giant shrug of the shoulders, a cosmic 'Whatever.'"[14]

Indeed. Imagine a blind man standing on the edge of a cliff who asks you, "Which way should I step?" Would it be best to respond, "I really shouldn't say that one direction is better than another, even though I believe I know"? Or imagine going to a doctor and hearing her say, "You have a malignant tumor spreading throughout your body. I believe I have the knowledge to cure it, but to say so seems arrogant, and risks being narrow-minded in regard to other options, even though everything in my training and experience convinces me they won't help. So I think it's best if I say nothing at all."[15]

Nonsense.

Perhaps the heart of our dilemma is our relationship with the very *idea* of truth. Our postmodern world, as philosopher

Richard Rorty has suggested, often thinks of truth as something to be made rather than found,[16] which is different from deciding that there is no truth to be found. It means that we tend to believe that all of our sources for what can be known—our scientific facts, our religious teachings, our society's beliefs, even our personal perceptions—are no more than the products of a highly creative and often imaginative interplay between ourselves and the cosmos.

But what if the Creator of the cosmos has spoken? The great commitment of the Christian faith is that there is a God, and he has not been silent. The omniscient God has broken through in self-revelation.

When the apostle Peter told the religious leaders of his day, "There is salvation in no one else [but Jesus Christ], for there is no other name under heaven given among mortals by which we must be saved" (Acts 4:12), he wasn't refusing them their right to believe differently, nor was he rejecting them socially or culturally. He was simply telling truth—referring to where salvation is found, as opposed to where it is not.

THE MILLIONS OF GOOD PEOPLE

But why can't salvation be found by at least all of the really good people, regardless of what faith they might embrace? How could a loving God send so many good non-Christians to hell?

Recently a young woman who had been attending our church for over a year asked to speak with me about her journey. As we talked, she readily shared how far she had come—now believing in the Bible and even in Jesus as God's Son. Coming from a deeply Jewish heritage, this was no small pilgrimage. Then came her stumbling block: "I can't believe my Jewish parents are in hell. I just can't believe those two wonderful people are not with God in heaven."

I know of only one pastoral response to such plaintive cries, but it is perhaps the most significant response that can be offered: "We must trust in the character of God."

Much of our relationship with God rests on our understanding of—and our faith in—his character. If God is God, he is completely fair and just. He will treat every person with complete and total love, and complete and total justice. This applies to those who have never heard the gospel, those who were not able to comprehend the gospel and those who seemed to reject the gospel. In this way the character of God, as revealed throughout the Bible, demands that the Christian be something of an "optimistic agnostic" when it comes to the salvation of others. Christ alone saves us, but God will make a perfect assessment of where someone stands in relation to Christ's saving grace.

> *"When we merely say that we are bad, the 'wrath' of God seems a barbarous doctrine; as soon as we perceive our badness, it appears inevitable, a mere corollary from God's goodness."*
>
> C. S. LEWIS,
> THE PROBLEM OF PAIN

Yet in saying this we must not lose sight of the reality of sin, our own sin-condition, and our need for Christ's saving grace. Perhaps no other reality is less understood in the modern world. We either project "sin" out into the world or trivialize the degree of its control over us.

Baptist minister Will Campbell, known for his disarmingly earthy approach to spirituality and life, described the Christian message in less than ten words: "We're all bastards but God loves us anyway."[17] We are keen to remember "God loves us," but we tend to forget the part about being less than holy.

The Bible teaches that no one is truly "good," and no one is in less of a broken relationship with God, and less in need of the *way* to God, than anyone else. This is behind Jesus' reply to a rich young man who asked what good thing he had to do to gain eternal life.

> "Why do you ask me about what is good?" Jesus replied.
> "There is only One who is good." (Matthew 19:17)

God made us to be in relationship with him. We break off that relationship through sin and rebellion. God offers to restore that relationship and repair the brokenness. The Bible teaches that it isn't God's desire that *anyone* should experience hell as a result of their broken relationship with him, but that *everyone* would receive the gift of eternal life in heaven through Christ (John 3:16-17; see also 1 Timothy 2:4; 2 Peter 3:9; 1 John 2:2). If we do that in this life, we can look forward to that relationship continuing on for eternity in heaven. If we choose *not* to return to God—never entering into that relationship—then we have set our course for eternity as well. Whatever choice we make in this life, God says at the end, "so be it." We will receive that which we desired. The choice is *real*, and truly ours to make.

C. S. Lewis once imagined a bus filled with inhabitants of hell who were allowed a visit to heaven. They didn't want to stay. His book *The Great Divorce* speaks to the divide between heaven and hell: the joyous hearts of those who chose God and the settled hearts of those who spurned him. God's final word regarding our settled choice in life will reflect the true disposition of our heart.

ONE WAY

So is there really just one way to God? Of course!

If my relationship with John were broken because of something *I* did, it would not matter if I spent my life trying to be in a good relationship with Rick. My problem is with *John*. The only way to deal with it is to deal with John and hope that he is gracious enough to forgive me.

Spiritually, our sin results in a broken relationship with a very specific Person. The reality of there being "one way" is little more than the reality of there being one God. There is only one relationship to be repaired.

The incredible nature of God's character is that he responds to this dilemma by taking it upon himself to reach out to each person. He is on a cosmic search and rescue mission that will not relent until *all* have had the opportunity to come freely to his side.

After all, he's after our hearts.

PART TWO

The Struggle
of Our Souls

S*oul* is a difficult word to define. In the Bible it refers to life, being, person or self. The word is translated literally as "to breathe," yet it refers not simply to the state of being "alive" but more to that part of life that is *most* alive, the part of our life that makes us most who we are as persons. Thus the soul distinguishes us from all other creatures.

There are three dimensions to existence: the physical, the psychosocial and the spiritual. A rock has a physical existence but nothing more. An animal has both a physical and psychosocial existence, for it is conscious and able to relate in certain ways to other beings. But only human beings have been given a physical, psychosocial and *spiritual* dimension. From the soul flows our identity as sons and daughters of God.

When God made us, he gave us a spark of the eternal, a slice of the divine. The soul is that unique element of life that reflects God's own image. Our souls enable us to do what only humans can do: respond and relate to God. The soul is the part within us that comes alive spiritually. Jesus said that those who cling to their life—their "soul," in the original language—would lose it, but those who would lose their life for his sake would gain it (Matthew 10:39, 16:25; Mark 8:35; Luke 9:24, 17:33; John 12:24). From the soul comes our hunger, our very yearning for God.

And the call of God is to love him with all of it.

We enter into a relationship with God by choosing to relate to him through Christ at the soul level. Then an ever-increasing acreage of the inner world is developed in love and devotion to God. Like a cavern that is excavated, opened and filled with light, the soul is meant to be filled increasingly with the living God.

Soul love is the basis of communion with God. We open ourselves to his presence and power, crying out with Moses "Now show me your glory," in order to speak with the Lord face to face, as a person speaks with a friend (see Exodus 33).

And yet, though God was willing to pass all of his goodness before his friend, and even proclaim his name to Moses, Moses was never allowed to encounter God *directly*. The face of God was to be hidden, for no one could see God and live.

Our souls ache for communion with God, yet we experience this restraint and feel estranged from him. As one disillusioned character in Jean Paul Sartre's play *The Devil and the Good Lord* exclaims:

> I prayed, I demanded a sign. I sent messages to Heaven, no reply. Heaven ignored my very name. Each minute I wonder what I could BE in the eyes of God. Now I know the answer: nothing. God does not see me, God does not hear me, God does not know me. You see this emptiness over our heads? That is God. You see this gap in the door? It is God. You see that hole in the ground? That is God again. Silence is God. Absence is God. God is the loneliness of man.[1]

We find it difficult to love God with our souls without seeing him. Often when we need communion with God the most, he seems most silent, most distant. Few struggles are as acute as the soul's search for God—desperately wanting his attention, only to find ourselves groping in the darkness, unable to hear his voice, unable to find his hand to clasp.

Three

THE DISTANCE OF GOD

Why, O LORD, do you stand far off?
Why do you hide yourself in times of trouble?
PSALM 10:1

John Crowe Ransom once observed that winter could be a season of the heart as much as a season of the year. Author and historian Martin Marty agreed. During and then after the death of his wife, Elsa, after a long illness, he experienced a "cry of absence." The Divine was distant, the sense of the sacred was remote. An emptiness invaded his soul, for God felt removed and aloof. The bright warmth of summer spirituality became lost in the long nights of winter's wasteland.[1]

We have all experienced the winter of the soul—the felt distance of God. It does not matter who you are or where you stand in relation to spiritual development.

Consider a young woman, attempting to follow God in obedience, walking the streets of the city she had just come to serve. She felt rejected by God, helpless and tempted to turn her back on her calling. Though she longed for God and desired to be used completely by him, she felt unable to pray—abandoned by God at her time of greatest need. "They say people in hell suffer eternal pain because of loss of God," she wrote. "In my soul, I feel just the terrible pain of loss, of God not wanting me, of God not being God, of God not really existing." The young woman was Mother Teresa.[2]

The Bible assures us that God is near.

> But you, O God, do see trouble and grief,
>> you consider it to take it in hand. . . .
> You hear, O LORD, the desire of the afflicted;
>> you encourage them, and you listen to their cry.
> (Psalm 10:14, 17)

Such verses give weight to the great theological doctrine of God's immanence, his presence and activity within creation and history.

So why do we often feel such distance?

There is great complexity to any interpersonal relationship. The dynamics of intimacy are multifaceted and often exist well beneath our consciousness. The felt distance of God must be engaged in light of God's immanence (he is indeed present), and his personal and relational nature. We can be physically present with someone and emotionally distant at the same time. God interacts with us in the context of an interpersonal relationship, and he longs to shape who we are. God is always there, and yet the same God comes and goes in relation to the ongoing development of our soul. God *can* seem distant, but always for a reason, beginning with the most counterintuitive reason imaginable: God can seem distant to us because we moved.

WE HAVE MOVED

We tend to put the distance we feel from God squarely on his shoulders, as if the burden of the relationship is on him. But our relationship with God, like any relationship, requires that we do our part to maintain intimacy.

My wife's sister became a Christian when she was young, yet at the tender age of seventeen began an eighteen-year battle with bulimia. During that time God seemed far removed from her plight. She would cry out for help, sending prayers to God, but by her own admission she never wanted God to respond in kind. God knew where to find her, she reasoned, but over time she realized that for God to draw near, she had to draw near to him.

So one Sunday morning she decided to go to a church. *It doesn't matter what church or denomination I go to,* she told herself. *I'll leave it in God's hands. The first church I come to, that's the one I'll attend.*

The first church she came to was a Greek Orthodox church. *Greek churches probably spoke Greek in church, so God can't have meant that one.* She drove on.

She came to a Baptist church and found herself the lone Anglo woman in a sea of shining black faces. Thinking that this "first church I come to" approach was not going to work, she turned to leave. Before she made it to the door, a woman stopped her and asked, "Where are you going, child?"

She wanted to say, "I'm going to the next church God brings me to." Instead, she said, "I'm waiting outside for a friend named Marilyn." How she came up with the name Marilyn, she had no idea.

"Marilyn who?" the woman kindly asked. "I might know her."

Without thinking, she said, "Marilyn Monroe." (She actually said that.)

"I don't know her," the woman said without skipping a beat. "Maybe someone here knows her." Then she proceeded to ask everyone standing in the foyer if they knew Marilyn Monroe. They didn't.

She then invited Judy to sit with her and her family. Judy did, and through that single service, she began her journey back to intimacy with God.

But the journey was hers to begin.

The ancient Celtic Christians spoke of going to "thin places" or seeking out "thin times" where God was close enough to envelope them in his love and presence. Key to their thinking was the importance of taking it upon themselves to *go* there.

When people tell me that God seems distant in their lives, "What are you doing to stay close?" is often my first question. A spiritual malady is at hand, and we need to seek out the cause of the trouble.

- Are you praying?

- Are you spending time reading and reflecting on the Bible in order to apply it to your life?

- Are you involved in worship?

- Are you connecting with people whose relationship with God challenges and encourages your own?

- Are you engaged in some kind of ministry to others?

- Are you carving out time for spiritually oriented reflection?

If the answer to any of these queries is "no," then there's no wonder that God feels distant. Our relationship with God *must* be nurtured and developed. We can begin a spiritual life, but we must also develop it. God continues to ask the question: "Who is he who will devote himself to be close to me?" (Jeremiah 30:21).

There are differences between religion, a personal relationship and an intimate relationship with Christ.[3] Religion is ritual and framework, worldview and dogma; relationship involves coming into community with a Person. Yet relationship alone only speaks to the nature of the relationship, not its depth. Intimacy comes in the pursuit of the relationship.

WE HAVE SINNED AGAINST HIM

God can also seem distant because we have sinned against him. The Bible teaches that when we sin, which we all do, our relationship with God is affected: "Your iniquities have separated you from your God; / your sins have hidden his face from you" (Isaiah 59:2).

Sin, at its heart, is an offense against a God of radical grace and unlimited forgiveness. His grace flows freely, but only toward those who own their sin, confessing it, mourning it and turning from it. If we harbor sin, we shouldn't wonder why God might seem removed. Unconfessed, unconfronted, unrepented sin disrupts our intimacy with God. It distances us from him in inescapable ways.

We often underestimate the cosmic scream that pierced creation at the Fall, a short word that refers to a deep and long scarring of the world through the sin of Adam and Eve. The intimacy for which we were created was not simply lost but violated. Sin divides. Sin betrays. At its heart, sin is opposed to community. It tears asunder that which was meant to be together.

Jesus experienced the most poignant distance caused by sin recorded in Scripture, crying "My God, my God, why have you forsaken me?" as he bore the sins of the world (Matthew 27:46), but despite the uniqueness of that terrible, glorious moment, we take from it a critical hope. The breach between our soul and the presence of God can often be mended through nothing more, but nothing less, than a prayer of confession.

WE HAVE NOT ALLOWED HIM TO COME NEAR

One of the tragic ironies of life is our tendency to keep God at bay, particularly at times when we need him most by our side. We respond like frenzied animals blinded by pain, lashing out at whoever rushes first to our aid. We simply are not open to his presence—not willing to have him come near and help. We refuse to yield to his insights and guidance. We're far too occupied by our attempts to save ourselves. God waits until we are willing to have him come to our rescue.

Sadly, some *never* let God draw near. One of the most poignant examples of this in all of Scripture was when Jesus approached the city of Jerusalem to celebrate the Passover. They would welcome him with shouts of "Hosanna!" ("Save us!"), but within a week they would reject him with cruel chants of "Crucify him."

And Jesus knew it.

As he approached Jerusalem and saw the city, he wept over it and said, "If you . . . had only known on this day what would bring you peace—but now it is hidden from your eyes . . . because you did not recognize the time of God's coming to you." (Luke 19:41-44)

Opening ourselves to God is a difficult process to navigate alone. We naturally tend to do all we can before seeking divine guidance, not to mention divine intervention. We need warning signs to alert us when we keep God at bay: conviction when sin erects its barriers; humility when our pride blocks our access to God; silence when our lives drown out the voice of God. None of these is universal, save one: the more we are overwhelmed by a matter, despite the temptation to strategize and maneuver, the more we should fall first to our knees.

WE HAVE ENTERED A DRY SEASON

Yet the Bible says more about the apparent distance of God than simply self-inflicted separation. Sometimes the perceived distance is a natural experience of the human condition. C. S. Lewis referred to this ebb and flow of our experience of God's presence as the law of undulation. To *undulate* means to move in waves, to go up and down. This movement is normal for us—not just emotionally but spiritually.

We have times when God seems close and intimate, and times when we feel he has left our lives completely. But we are being unrealistic if we expect always to feel intimate with God in the intermingling of our spirituality and our emotions. And unrealistic expectations are relationally destructive.

I once knew a newlywed couple who declared they would never lose the romance of their fledgling relationship. Unlike others, they would maintain the fires of feeling perpetually "in love." Within two years they divorced. They could not withstand the inevitable slide of romance into reality. Lasting relationships, on the other hand, mature. They do not simply survive the waning of romance; instead, they expect and commit to something richer and of more depth than mere romantic feelings.

We tend to think that intimacy, even intimacy with God, can be gauged by *feeling*. Do I *feel* close to God? Do I *feel* spiritual? The reality is that authentic spirituality has more to do with how we *respond* to emotions than it does with a given emotional state. There will be times we feel high or low, near or far. Those feelings may have very little to do with where we actually are with God. The real state of our souls does not rest on how we feel but on who God is, who we are in relation to God and who we are *becoming*.

Consequently, faith is often forged during the remote times, the winters of the heart. Notice this dynamic at work in the following prayer of David:

> How long, O LORD? Will you forget me forever?
>> How long will you hide your face from me?
> How long must I wrestle with my thoughts
>> And every day have sorrow in my heart? . . .
> But I trust in your unfailing love;
>> my heart rejoices in your salvation.
> I will sing to the LORD,
>> For he has been good to me. (Psalm 13:1-2, 5-6)

Douglas Steere writes of a "rugged persistence" in coming to God during feelings of separation, citing an event in the history of America's oldest college, William and Mary. Closed throughout the Civil War, the school was expected by many never to reopen. Yet each day for five years an old custodian rang the bells of the ghost school as though it still lived. At the end of five years, he rang them for a reopening that vindicated his vigil of faith.[4] Faith in God requires a similar persistence to plough through the dry seasons of life.

But yet another dynamic can be at play during times of felt distance from God.

WE HAVE NOT SEEN WHERE HE IS

"Surely the LORD is in this place, and I was not aware of it" was the conclusion Jacob drew from his startling vision of the ladder to heaven (Genesis 28:10-17). Building off of this biblical confession, Philip Yancey asks, "If we miss God's presence in the world, could it be that we have looked in the wrong places, or perhaps looked without seeing the grace before our eyes?"[5] There can be little doubt that God can seem distant simply because we do not see where he is.

The king of Aram had sent soldiers and chariots to surround the city where Elisha was staying. Elisha's servant woke up, saw the army and ran to Elisha in a frenzied panic, crying, "What shall we do!"

> "Don't be afraid," the prophet answered. "Those who are with us are more than those who are with them."
>
> And Elisha prayed, "O LORD, open his eyes so he may see." Then the LORD opened the servant's eyes, and he looked and saw the hills full of horses and chariots of fire all around Elisha. (2 Kings 6:15-17)

Such vision seems beyond us, yet it is possible, and the ancient insight of the Christian Celts can again be of help. Avoiding pantheism (the idea that God *is* everything), as well as panentheism (the belief that God is *in* everything), they saw God *through* everything. A sense of God's presence informed their daily life to such a degree that any moment and any task could become the time and place for an encounter with the living God. They simply assumed that God was present, and they lived accordingly.

Consider the daily task of rising and starting a fire. They would accompany the act with the following prayer:

I will kindle my fire this morning
In the presence of the holy angels of heaven.[6]

Then throughout the day with every endeavor—from the milking of a cow to the cooking of a meal—they would acknowledge the presence of God. At the end of the day, as they banked the fire for the night, they would offer a last prayerful recognition of God's immanence:

The sacred Three
To save
To shield
To surround
The hearth
The house
The household
This eve
This night
And every night
Each single night. Amen.[7]

To the Celtic soul God was seen as revealing himself in every occurrence of life. John Scotus Eriguena (810-877), arguably the greatest thinker the Celtic church produced, liked to speak of the world as God's theophany (visible appearance or manifestation). These theophanies were deeply personal, as is expressed in the last stanza of the eighth-century "Deer's Cry," more popularly known as St. Patrick's breastplate, perhaps the greatest of all Celtic hymns:

> Christ with me, Christ before me, Christ behind me;
> Christ within me, Christ beneath me, Christ above me;
> Christ to right of me, Christ to left of me;
> Christ in my lying, Christ in my sitting, Christ in my
>   rising;
> Christ in the heart of all who think of me,
> Christ on the tongue of all who speak to me,
> Christ in the eye of all who see me,
> Christ in [the] ear of all who hear me.[8]

This was the lesson of the Celtic soul: *they opened their eyes to God.*

Still there remains to be discussed the least considered dynamic of God's "distance": God seems distant because he is.

BECAUSE HE IS

The willful detachment of God is one of the most unexplored themes in Scripture, yet it appears often. Jesus delayed his visit to the bereaved sisters Mary and Martha when their brother Lazarus died. Jesus isolated himself from the disciples after sending them into the midst of a storm-tossed sea. These were deliberate separations meant for instruction and special action. Faith was being built, and God's distance was the brick and mortar.

In the Old Testament, distance was designed not only to teach about God but to protect the people from his holiness as they learned how to relate to him. Distance was used to convey the reality that God was not to be treated casually. Thus Mount Sinai was covered in darkness, and the people were not allowed to ascend with Moses as he met with God. God made his place of meeting with his people first in the Promised Land (Israel), then in a particular city (Jerusalem) and then in a particular place (the temple). Even the temple was separated by degrees of holiness: the outer court, the sanctuary and the Holy of Holies. The faithful were expected to exercise increasing caution as they drew near to the meeting place of the living God.

And in this was God's care and concern, for the fire that warms is also the fire that can burn.

OPENING YOUR EYES

Try this seemingly trivial but potentially enlightening exercise: Stop reading, and look for two things that contain the color green.

Maybe the clothes someone near you is wearing, the paint on the ceiling, the wallpaper on the walls, the carpet or tile on the floor—any two things that are green. What happened?

You changed how you looked at what was around you.

For lack of a better term, you created a green mindset. And when you created that green mindset, you began to see green in places you probably had not noticed the color before. The reason is simple: we tend to see what we sensitize ourselves to see.[9]

There are countless ways in which God can seem distant, and sometimes he *is* distant. We have removed ourselves from intimacy with him, or our sin has driven a wedge between us. Sometimes he has removed himself as a gift—for our instruction or our protection. But many times we just aren't aware of him. He's there, but we're going through a down-cycle in our spiritual or emotional life, and we don't feel him at our side—so we go with our feelings. Or we're trying to save ourselves, and we don't open ourselves up to him, though he is eager to lend a hand. Or we think we're facing the world alone, unaware that the hills are full of angels.

We must open our eyes, for "surely the LORD is in this place" (Genesis 28:16).

Four

THE SILENCE OF GOD

My God, my God, why have you forsaken me?
Why are you so far from saving me,
so far from the words of my groaning?
O my God, I cry out by day, but you do not answer.
PSALM 22:1-2

Few Christians have chronicled their struggle with God more poignantly than C. S. Lewis. The famed author was deeply in love with his wife, Joy. Though they met and married late in life, few romances bloom as theirs did. Not long after their relationship began, she was diagnosed with cancer. She endured a long and terrible season of illness before she died.

Lewis wrote about his feelings following Joy's death in a series of notebooks that were later published as *A Grief Observed* just before his own death in 1963. His most telling observation? The silence of God.

No one ever told me that grief felt so like fear. I am not afraid, but the sensation is like being afraid. The same fluttering in the stomach, the same restlessness. . . . On the rebound one passes into tears and pathos. Maudlin tears. I almost prefer the moments of agony. These are at least clean and honest. . . .

Meanwhile, where is God? . . . When you are happy, so happy that you have no sense of needing Him . . . if you remember yourself and turn to Him with gratitude and praise, you will be—or so it feels—welcomed with open arms. But go to Him when your need is desperate, when all other help is vain, and what do you find? A door slammed in your face, and a sound of bolting and double bolting on the inside. After that, silence. You may as well turn away. The longer you wait, the more emphatic the silence will become. . . .

Why is He so present a commander in our time of prosperity and so very absent a help in time of trouble?[1]

Many of us have experienced the silence of God. We cry out to God, and there seems to be no answer. We pray, pouring out our hearts, only to hear the words echo back without a reply.

The maddening thing is that we have been conditioned to expect a direct relation between input and output. If we work a certain number of hours, we will reach a certain level of success. If we place our children in the right schools, enroll them in the right programs and practice the proper procedures, they will turn out as hoped for. If we invest our money strategically and wisely, we will receive a fair return on our investment.

When we cry out to God and nothing happens, how can we help but feel that something's not quite right—and that the problem is with the Listener? Few things are more damaging to a relationship than a sense of not being heard or responded to. It's as if we don't matter, that there is no genuine concern. If God is calling for our soul, and we are attempting to connect with him at that level, there seems no place—no excuse—for silence.

The silence, however, is seldom permanent. Lewis later wrote these words: "I have gradually been coming to feel that the door is no longer shut and bolted. . . . [I was like] the drowning man who can't be helped because he clutches and grabs."[2]

So what was he clutching and grabbing? What was he missing in what first seemed like silence? Perhaps the most penetrating question is simply this: What happens when we call out to God?

According to the Bible, three things.

GOD HEARS, CARES, RESPONDS

When we pray, God hears us. The Bible states in no uncertain terms that "this is the confidence we have in approaching God: . . . he hears us" (1 John 5:14). When we pray, whether by spoken word, ritual or quiet anguish, our prayers ascend unencumbered to God's presence. But that's not all.

When we pray, *God cares.* What we attempt to convey is more important to him than we could possibly imagine. The Bible asserts this as well: "Let him [God] have all your worries and cares, for he is always thinking about you and watching everything that concerns you" (1 Peter 5:7 LB). Notice the emphasis: God is concerned not simply with his grand plan but with our cares and concerns. When it comes to prayer, God's empathy knows no bounds.

But it is the Bible's third declaration that perplexes us. When we pray, *God answers.* The Bible is emphatic: there is no such thing as an unanswered prayer. "You say, 'He does not respond to people's complaints.' But God speaks again and again, though people do not recognize it" (Job 33:13-14 NLT).

Now you may be thinking, *That isn't true. I specifically prayed for a Maserati sports car, and it's not sitting in my driveway, so I know God doesn't answer every prayer.* I know—I've prayed that one too.

Or you may say, "Once I prayed that I would get to work on time—that was it, no big deal, no sweat off God's brow—and I got a flat tire."

More seriously, you may resonate with Lewis's feelings after his wife passed away. When you hear someone casually toss out that God answers every prayer, you say, "Listen, that's just not true. And I have the *experience* to prove it."

But the Bible doesn't back down when challenged on this.

It stands by the declaration that God hears, cares *and* responds. Always.

So what is happening with God's answer?

In our struggle with God's perceived silence we must take into account an idea that is often alien to our sensibilities: that a prayer was not answered in the way we *wanted* it answered or thought it *should* have been answered, doesn't mean that an answer did not come directly from God. God promises to answer every prayer; *how* he chooses to answer is his affair. Consider the following ways a clear response from God might be mistaken for silence.

MISTAKEN FOR SILENCE: NO

The first is the most obvious. Sometimes God's answer is simply "No." What we ask for, no matter how well-intentioned, could be inappropriate. Yet we often refuse to listen to God's no, insisting instead that God has yet to answer. It is often beyond our thinking to imagine God denying our requests.

Once Jesus and his followers were traveling to Jerusalem. One of the cities they journeyed through was Samaria, so some went ahead to arrange a place with local inhabitants for Jesus and the rest of the disciples to stay. What happened next is interesting:

> The people there did not welcome him. . . . When the disciples James and John saw this, they asked, "Lord, do you want us to call fire down from heaven to destroy them?" (Luke 9:53-54)

These two disciples sincerely felt that their question made perfect sense in terms of what had transpired. But did Jesus answer, "Sure, guys, let's smoke 'em"?

Jesus turned on them: "Of course not!" (Luke 9:55 The Message).

God cares deeply about us and hears every request, but that doesn't mean his answer can't still be "No." This becomes particularly clear to me when I think of my role as a father. Nobody loves my children more than I do. But sometimes when they ask for something, the answer must be—for *their* sake— a firm and deliberate no. More times than not, they don't have a clue as to why. It makes perfect sense in their minds to stay up all night, to eat pizza for every meal, to invest a significant amount of our financial resources into the profit margin of the local mall, and to establish a secondary residence in Orlando. I've seen this lessen as they mature. Their requests are more informed as they learn to apply the values by which they have been raised. Yet still they make occasional requests that reflect pockets of immaturity and require a "No" response.

So it is with our souls in relation to prayer. We often make requests that cannot be granted. But we can be assured that God's operative stance toward us is shameless devotion. Even when pain erupts, tragic events are allowed to continue or God denies our requests, we can rest assured that we have been granted a greater blessing—or kept from a deeper, more lasting pain.

And God's no is seldom left to itself. The answer often goes further. When Paul repeatedly begged God to remove his "thorn in the flesh," the answer was "No." But there was more: "[God] said to me, 'My grace is sufficient for you, for my power is made perfect in weakness'" (2 Corinthians 12:9). The purpose behind God's refusal and the ramifications it holds for our life are met by the direct presence and power of God. The fullest sense of God's reply is "No, but I'm here . . . and it will be OK. Trust me."

MISTAKEN FOR SILENCE: NOT NOW

But "No" is not the only response from God that can be mistaken for silence. Sometimes when he seems silent he is saying, "Not now." When we ask God for something, we are looking for it at once. We have a predetermined timetable. If God were to say, "Not now—the timing is neither right nor best," it would be natural to interpret his answer as silence.

What adds to the difficulty of "Not now" is that we are so used to instant gratification. We can't imagine a life without express lanes, ATMs, faxes, e-mail and instant messaging. We're used to getting what we want when we want it, which makes "Later" or "Not now" only slightly easier to hear than "No."

But God's delay should not be confused with his denial, much less his silence. He always has reasons for saying "Not now," and we should greet such delays with trust and patience. The willingness to wait in prayer and let God's timetable unfold is behind the Message translation of Romans 8:22-25: "Waiting does not diminish us, any more than waiting diminishes a pregnant mother. We are enlarged in the waiting."

Besides, we may not be ready for what God would say. The delay may have less to do with the timing of events than the timing of our soul's growth. Dallas Willard writes that we may have so little clarity on what a word from God should be like, and so little competence in dealing with it, that such a word would only add to our confusion, even "when it would otherwise be entirely appropriate and helpful."[3]

As I write these words, I am waiting for God's guidance on a host of issues that will determine my steps for the next season of my life. My petition is clear and direct, but the complexities that surround whatever resolution he chooses to bring overwhelm me. The shadows are maddening. Why won't he just tell me or show me!

My sense is that the answer is there, but I am not ready to receive his words. There is something he is doing *in* me that apparently must come before he reveals what he is going to do *with* me. So I watch and try to cooperate as he moves and shapes pieces of my life—both internally and externally. I'm waiting in what sounds like silence, but in truth God is on the loose.

MISTAKEN FOR SILENCE: DEEP CALLING TO DEEP

A third response from God that can be mistaken for silence is the most difficult to grasp. Perhaps the best way to introduce it is through the words of Psalm 42:

> As the deer pants for streams of water,
>   so my soul pants for you, O God.
> My soul thirsts for God, for the living God. . . .
> My tears have been my food
>   day and night,
> while men say to me all day long,
>   "Where is your God?" (Psalm 42:1-3)

Here is someone hungering for a word from God. He alludes to a difficult time, a season where he has been calling out to God in the midst of pain, grief or confusion. From all angles it appears as if God is silent to his cries. But notice what he goes on to write:

> Why are you downcast, O my soul?
>   Why so disturbed within me?
> Put your hope in God. . . .
> My soul is downcast within me;
>   therefore I will remember you. . . .
> Deep calls to deep
>   in the roar of your waterfalls. (Psalm 42:5-7)

The psalmist comes to see that there is no silence; the answer coming from God is deeper than words. God is present, and speaking, but what he's saying isn't resting on the surface waters of life. This is a season where deep is calling to deep or, as Thomas Kelly phrases it, a time of going "down into the recreating silences."[4]

When I was nineteen years old and in college, I was invited to a weekend party at a nearby university. My friend Phil was going, and he encouraged me to come along. I wanted to go and tried to make it happen, but I couldn't get away.

Four people left without me on a Friday afternoon. Two days later, as they returned to campus, a car from the opposite flow of traffic crossed the dividing line and flew headfirst into their car. All four were killed instantly.

I first heard the news late that Sunday night. I left my dorm, walked over to the nearby athletic complex, hopped a locked fence and sat in the empty football stadium under a moonlit sky. I grieved for my friend; I thought of the brevity of life and how close I had come to being killed. I remember crying out to God to help me sort it all out, to make sense of it all. To talk to me . . . to say something . . . anything!

Silence.

In truth, it was the deepest conversation we had ever had. God was moving within me, communing and communicating with me on levels that I had never opened to him before. That night was the first of many such conversations—some even more traumatic. Within four months I became a Christian.

> *"Let none expect from silence anything but a direct encounter with the Word of God."*
>
> DIETRICH BONHOEFFER,
> *LIFE TOGETHER*

Perhaps it's not silence we're encountering while we seek God, but rather a pregnant pause—a prompting to engage in personal reflection so that the deepest of answers, the most profound of responses, can be given and received.

In an article in the magazine *Fast Company,* the chess master and much sought-after mentor Bruce Pandolfini discusses how he works with his students:

> My lessons consist of a lot of silence. I listen to other teachers, and they're always talking. . . . I let my students think. If I do ask a question and I don't get the right answer, I'll rephrase the question—and wait. I never give the answer. Most of us really don't appreciate the power of silence. Some of the most effective communication—between student and teacher, between master players—takes place during silent periods.[5]

Could this be how God mentors us? Is God's apparent silence the method of a Master Teacher? When I go through seasons where God's answers do not come quickly or on the surface of things—but the way God interacts with my prayers draws me into deeper trust, dependence and obedience—the answers I find radically transcend what I initially sought to find.

- I get introduced to sin that I need to confront.

- I recognize patterns of behavior I need to break.

- I gain insights into who I am that I didn't have before.

- I discover a depth of relationship with God that I have never before experienced.

Such revelations are worth the silence.

Kathleen Norris allows her students to make all the noise they want, but then she calls on them to "make silence." Reflecting on the experience, her elementary-age pupils note that when they were silent, they felt as though they were "waiting for something." One wrote, "Silence is me sleeping waiting to wake up." Perhaps the most profound observation comes from a little girl who said, "Silence reminds me to take my soul with me wherever I go."[6]

Few statements could be more profound. We think of a word from God as the soul's main sustenance, but silence is a true compatriot not simply for where it leads but for what it affords: space for God to speak beyond the answers we seek.

"It is no surprise," writes Frederick Buechner, "that the Bible uses hearing, not seeing, as the predominant image for the way human beings know God."[7] Perhaps this deeper communion is behind the concept of *vigils* (waiting), the ancient name for extended prayers given while one might normally be sleeping. It also suggests why the first word of St. Benedict's Rule for monasteries is *listen*.

Before even these insights came the ancient desert tradition of Christianity. Alan Jones writes of men and women entering the literal desert even as they embraced a "desert" of the spirit—at once "a place of silence, waiting, and temptation" and "a place of revelation, conversion, and transformation." According to the desert tradition, "empty" places such as the desert were actually full, for in the deadening silence of such experiences, people were known to be reborn.[8]

This was certainly the experience of Jesus, who was led by the Holy Spirit into the desert to begin his ministry, and then led into the desert again to end it. Jesus' cry from the cross "My God, my God, why have you forsaken me?" speaks to the separation within the Trinity as Jesus took on the world's sin, but it also serves as a "silent" reminder to Jesus of a "deeper magic" that causes death itself to work backward. As Larry Crabb notes, Jesus screamed in agony "God, where are you?" and God seemed to say nothing. But deep was calling to deep, and in his reconciling the world to himself Jesus heard the voice of God in the depths of his heart.[9]

I can only wonder what his silence holds for me.

A CONFEDERATE PRAYER

My family has been Carolinian on both sides for generations, making me the product of a fast-disappearing Southern culture of sweetened iced-tea, two meats at supper, sitting on your porch to watch the cars go by, saying "Yes Ma'am" and "No Sir," and bringing meals to those who are sick.

The southern world of even the near-past cannot be understood apart from the Civil War. A pathos came to the surface during those years that crystallized long-standing traditions and ideals. Though often marred by the blight of racism, students of the era know the divide between the states was multifaceted, and the South had its share of people of authentic faith who despised slavery.

As "the cause," as the war came to be known in the South, began to fail—in the midst of what surely seemed like the silence of God—a Confederate soldier composed a simple prayer.

I asked God for strength, that I might achieve,
I was made weak, that I might learn humbly to obey.

I asked for health, that I might do great things,
I was given infirmity, that I might do better things.

I asked for riches, that I might be happy,
I was given poverty, that I might be wise.

I asked for power, that I might have the praise of men,
I was given weakness, that I might feel the need of God.

I asked for all things, that I might enjoy life,
I was given life, that I might enjoy all things.

I got nothing that I asked for, but everything that I had hoped for.
Almost despite myself, my unspoken prayers were answered.
I am, among all men, most richly blessed.[10]

That soldier experienced the voice of God, and listened to every word. A struggle? Yes. But this prayer was written on the other side of his struggle. He understood that God never met him with silence.

He had only to listen.

PART THREE

The Struggle of Our Minds

M*ind*, or *intellect*, refers to our thinking, the use of our reason and cognitive capabilities to interpret and understand the world around us. To the command in Deuteronomy 6:5 which characterized human devotion to God as a matter of heart, soul and strength, Jesus added the mind.

Many biblical scholars consider this addition only marginally significant. The terms used in this way form an idiom that points out the comprehensive nature of full devotion. But the question remains: Why did Jesus add to an idiom that already accomplished its intent? At the very least, Jesus wanted to make sure that when we thought of giving our total selves to him, we would not leave behind our minds.

We tend to think of spiritual things in terms of feeling (emotion and heart) or obedience (acts and rituals). What we don't tend to think of is our thoughts—our worldview and our rational faculties. Yet these aspects of ourselves cannot be separated from the call to love God wholly. As the apostle Paul reminds us, we are to "take captive every thought to make it obedient to Christ" (2 Corinthians 10:5).

Yet thoughts do not fall into submission with ease. They wander, losing their way and falling into fantasy. Most of all, they question. We insist on fitting God within the limits of our intellect, often piercing ourselves (knowingly or not) with Ockham's razor—William of Ockham's idea that what is most readily apparent to us must be true. Even more ingrained is Immanuel Kant's call for a "religion within the limits of reason alone," which supposes that we can only trust in what can be analyzed or experienced with our senses.

But God is beyond our mental faculties, thrusting religion beyond the limits of our reason. The wisdom of God is often foolishness to the minds of men and women, and the mystery of God is by its very definition outside of reason's capacity to understand.

But I want to understand. And to love God with my mind I *need* to understand.

And that's the struggle.

Five

THE FOOLISHNESS OF GOD

The adventures may be mad,
but the adventurer must be sane.
G. K. CHESTERTON,
THE MAN WHO WAS THURSDAY

Strolling through the Vincent van Gogh museum in Amsterdam, I stumbled on a disarmingly simple oil on canvas that has since hung prominently in the gallery of my mind. A Bible opened to Isaiah 53 lies next to a well-worn copy of Émile Zola's *La Joie de Vivre* on a wooden table. An extinguished candlestick—a typical symbol of death in the seventeenth-century Dutch *vanitas* tradition—is in the background, suggesting the fleeting nature of human existence.

The Bible is uniformly recognized by art historians as belonging to van Gogh's father, Theodorus, a minister whose love for the great prophet Isaiah was widely known. Zola's *La Joie de Vivre* was an example of French naturalist literature. Together they speak to van Gogh's lifelong attempt to reconcile his traditional Christian heritage to modern sensibilities.

It was a reconciliation he was never to achieve.

The problem van Gogh wrestled with is shared by many and, as it was with the great Dutch painter, runs deeper than reconciling the ancient to the contemporary. What is the place of the spiritual in a world that is overwhelmingly materialistic? We live in the context of what Richard John Neuhaus has termed a "naked public square," meaning a culture where discourse and conduct have been stripped of religious insight and influence.[1] In America, law and politics have so trivialized religious devotion that individuals are forced to act—at least in public—as if their faith doesn't matter.[2] As Page Smith once blithely noted, "God is not a proper topic for discussion, but 'lesbian politics' is."[3]

This void of religious contribution has made faith seem less "real" than other concepts and enterprises, particularly as we have tended to gauge truth by what can be empirically verified. Faith is not tangible and therefore, in this world, not relevant. As such, faith is not simply "foolishness to Gentiles" (1 Corinthians 1:23) but often foolishness to believers.

And the Bible doesn't help, at least at first glance.

A man who seems to enjoy his fair share of wine is told to build a boat. A really big one. In the desert. And then two of every animal is said to be stowed away in order to survive a cataclysmic flood.

A pre-Viagra seventy-five-year-old man is called to get his wife pregnant and start a nation. And, we are told, he does.

A young girl offers to water a stranger's camels and is offered instantly by her family to a wandering nomad in order to perpetuate the people of God. Her reaction? "Okay."

So far we have not progressed beyond the first of the sixty-six books in the Bible. And it doesn't get any better. Such examples led philosopher Søren Kierkegaard to see Christianity as a "leap in the dark," a letting go of experience and rationality in order to embrace what is beyond experience and reason.

This was the dilemma facing Boromir in the first part of J. R. R. Tolkien's trilogy *The Lord of the Rings*. The great Council of Elrond meets to determine what to do with the Ring of the Dark Lord, which fate had brought into their midst. It is decided that their one hope, against all rational thought, is to bring the ring to the Fire of Mount Doom, the very point of the ring's origin. Boromir, the valiant warrior from the city of Gondor who represents the race of men, speaks:

> I do not understand all this. . . . Why do you speak ever of hiding and destroying? Why should we not think that the Great Ring has come in to our hands to serve us in the very hour of need? . . . Let the Ring be your weapon, if it has such power as you say. Take it and go forth to victory!

The older and wiser Elrond reminds Boromir that the ring is altogether evil; using it against the Dark Lord would cause its bearer to become as the Dark Lord himself. Boromir submits to the Council, but not in his mind. As the company begins its journey, he confronts Frodo the ring-bearer, and once again raises the subject of using the ring.

> "Were you not at the Council?" answered Frodo. . . . "We cannot use it, and what is done with it turns to evil."
>
> "So you go on, . . . all these folk have taught you to say so. . . . Yet often I doubt if they are wise. . . . It is mad not to use it. . . . How I would drive the hosts of Mordor, and all men would flock to my banner! . . . The only plan that is proposed to us is that a halfling should walk blindly into Mordor and offer the Enemy every chance of recapturing it for himself. Folly!" [4]

But it isn't folly. It is supreme wisdom—a wisdom running counter to that which intellect alone could muster.

The apostle Paul reminds the church at Corinth "how foolish the message of the cross sounds" on its surface. But God has already determined, "I will destroy human wisdom" because it proves "to be useless nonsense" according to his standards. God's " 'foolish' plan . . . is far wiser than the wisest of human plans" (1 Corinthians 1:18-20, 25 NLT).

Loving God with all of our mind, however, takes more than simple faith in God. Foundational Christian beliefs have lately come under siege through the shared intellectual endeavors of the world around us.

A FORTRESS UNDER SEIGE

During the thirteenth century, few things matched the importance of the castle. Its military, political, social, economic and cultural roles were paramount. Castles were developed in tenth-century continental Europe as private fortresses of timber and earthwork, brought to England by the Normans and redesigned using stone in the eleventh and twelfth centuries. The Syrian crusades exposed Northern Europe to new possibilities in engineering, so that by the end of the thirteenth century the medieval castle had reached the pinnacle of its development. Then in the fourteenth century, and increasingly in the fifteenth, a single product spread through Europe and led to the castle's decline.

Gunpowder. Suddenly castles were falling with astonishing speed to heavy stone balls fired from iron cannons. What was once deemed impervious suddenly proved vulnerable to a newly developed source of power.

As gunpowder firing cannon balls ended the age of castles, so the volleys of modern thought provided a new source of explanation and have decimated the fortress of faith. Of particular damage were those shots lofted by Copernicus, Darwin and Freud.

Copernicus and the cosmological attack. Copernicus (1473-1543) observed the heavens and determined that the universe did not revolve around the earth; rather the earth orbited the sun. At the time, the Christian church considered any understanding of the universe as other than earth-centered to be heresy.

The church's position was, of course, wrong.

Now, the Bible wasn't wrong, only a skewed assumption that the earth needed to be at the center of creation in order to uphold the special nature of God's creation on earth. But religious pronouncements on matters of public discourse have been automatically suspect ever since, and modern cosmologists now speak to issues of faith and philosophy with greater authority than priests and theologians.

Charles Darwin and the biological attack. Charles Darwin's (1809-1882) assault on the foundations of Christian thought was not cosmological but biological—or perhaps more accurately, anthropological. In *Origin of Species*, this minister's son contended that the origin of humankind could be accounted for in ways other than direct divine creation, namely natural selection. Despite the highly suspect assertions of Darwin's theory of evolution, the very idea of an explanation of human origins rooted in science rather than religion proved compelling.[5] Here was a mechanistic universe in which God did not exist, or at least did not intrude. Once the crown of creation, humankind was now "an accident" of impersonal forces.

Consider the staggering nature of these two volleys alone: First, earth was not the center of the universe, and now human beings were not the apex of creation. With the walls severely weakened, a third wave of assaults came whistling through the air.

Sigmund Freud and the psychological attack. The French philosopher Voltaire wrote in 1770, *"Se Dieu n'existait pas, il faudrait l'inventer"* ("If God did not exist, it would be necessary to invent him"). Sigmund Freud (1856-1939) later maintained that God does not exist; he is nothing but a projection of our desires, and the very *idea* of a human soul is conditioned by our desires. We want there to be a God, so we imagine such a Being.[6] There was now a seemingly intellectually satisfying explanation for spiritual conviction without an appeal to religious faith.

Intriguingly, Freud noted that the church has done little more than retreat from his assertion and other assaults. Rather than engage these challenges to a Christian worldview through the exercise of a rigorous intellect, the church denounced and denied, leaving faithful believers with scant resources as they encountered these challenges in the marketplace of ideas. The church abdicated its authority in public truth, and science was only too eager to assume the throne.

Little wonder that in our own day, doubt runs rampant even in the most ancient fortresses of faith and devotion. Near the end of a Monastic Institute marked by lectures on the loss of faith in American society, an anguished young Trappist said, "But what of loss of faith within the monastery itself?"[7]

THE ROLE OF REASON

A great danger in modern thought, one that many postmoderns have found bankrupt and have quickly cast aside, is the temptation to reduce the world to rational categories.

Many cling to the notion that if something cannot be gauged by the scientific method or grasped by the processes of rational thought, it cannot be real—or at least meaningful.

This is different from what Mark Noll chronicles in his book *The Scandal of the Evangelical Mind.* Modern evangelicals "are the spiritual descendants of leaders and movements distinguished by probing, creative, fruitful attention to the mind."[8] Evangelicals are scandalized by their failure to embrace this heritage. Noll and others rightly call Christians to develop a life of the mind, to think deeply and Christianly about the whole of life.

"Casual thought went with casual dress."
MICHAEL LEWIS, *NEXT*

No doubt many intellectual dilemmas arise not because we think too much but because we think too little. The greater struggle is to see reason for what it is—not a *source* for truth but a *test* for truth.[9] If Christianity is true, it will stand under any amount of intellectual scrutiny. Yet reason is limited in what it brings to the table of spiritual reality. Reason by itself cannot address the mysterious, the transcendent, the paradoxical and often the aesthetic. It leaves little room for a God beyond our five senses, yet by definition God is *supra*rational, meaning *beyond* reason. As Martin Luther counseled, "Faith should close its eyes and should not judge or decide according to what it feels or sees."[10] This is very different than being *non*rational or *ir*rational; God is not alien to reason but rather simply larger than reason. Faith is not so much a leap in the dark as a journey *toward* the light.

Yet the reality of doubt remains, and here the struggle to comprehend God is most keenly felt.

THE REALITY OF DOUBT

"Doubt," Os Guinness reminds us, "is not primarily an abstract philosophical or theological question, nor a state of morbid spiritual or psychological anguish. At its most basic, doubt is a matter of truth, trust and trustworthiness. Can we trust God? Are we sure? How can we be sure?" In this light, doubt is far from unbelief, and even for the believer, nothing to be ashamed of. "To believe," Guinness continues, "is to be 'in one mind' about accepting something as true; to disbelieve is to be 'in one mind' about rejecting it. To doubt is to waver between the two, to believe and disbelieve at once and so to be 'in two minds.'" [11] And we all have doubt. Frederick Buechner once noted that if you don't have any doubts, "you are either kidding yourself or asleep." [12]

My doubts started early. [13] At the ripe old age of nine, it dawned on me that I was a Christian because my parents were Christians, or at least held a Christian worldview and disposition. Like a thunderbolt from the blue, it hit me: *That's why I believed it all; I had been raised to believe it!* That, of course, did not make it true; my preadolescent brain quickly surmised that if I had been born in India, I would have been raised a Hindu. It would have been Hinduism that I would have believed and accepted. If I had been born in Iran, my parents would have raised me to accept the Muslim faith. I remember panicking: what if I wasn't born in the right country! My eternal destiny suddenly seemed to rest on whether my family of origin was geographically correct.

I went to my mother, innocently working in the kitchen and unaware of my spiritual crisis. "Mom, why are we Christians? You did, like, check it out first, didn't you? How do you know we're believing the right religion?"

She did not dismiss me, or give me a quick "Don't worry" kind of reply that would have trivialized my question. She knew me well enough to know that I was serious about the question, and how she answered me could decide my spiritual future. She also resonated with the question, for though I did not know it at the time, she had yet to fully embrace the Christian faith herself.

So she did something unusual. She said, "Jim, your father and I have looked at all of the faiths of the world, and have determined that Christianity is the right religion. It's not just about where we live. But you have to come to that in your own mind. So you are welcome to look into all of the world's religions and come to your own conclusions. And if, at the end, you want to go to a different church or believe something else, you may."

When she said that to me, two things happened. First, I heaved a sigh of relief. They had apparently done their homework (I had not given them credit for being as reflective about the matter as I had been), and I was free to pursue my questions without fear of retribution. There was something comforting, even reassuring, about such freedom.

My parents taught me that doubt itself is not wrong; it is simply the fuel that energizes faith as we seek understanding. As such, doubt is a developmental stage that humans are guaranteed to experience throughout their faith journey. Or as C. S. Lewis once wrote to a friend:

> I feel an amused recognition when you describe those moments at wh. one feels "How cd. I—I, of all people— ever have come to believe this cock and bull story." I think they will do us no harm. Aren't they just the reverse side of one's just recognition that the truth is amazing?[14]

The key is where we allow our doubt to take us.

THE STORY OF THOMAS

One of the most misunderstood characters in Scripture is the man who will forever be known as "doubting" Thomas. In truth, Thomas wanted to believe. He simply struggled with belief as a believer.

The story of Thomas begins at the very onset of Jesus' ministry, when Jesus was pulling together the men and women who would form his inner circle of followers. Thomas was one of the chosen Twelve (Luke 6:12-16). Amid earthy laborers, militant revolutionaries, disreputable financial players and one certified two-faced scoundrel was a man who *wanted* to believe but struggled. Jesus called, and Thomas answered.

Thomas proved fiercely loyal to Jesus. As Jesus began making waves with his miracles and teachings, the religious establishment began to feel threatened—to the point that when Jesus came to Judea, they tried to kill him. Jesus moved on to another city, but when his friend Lazarus became dangerously ill, Lazarus's sisters, Mary and Martha, asked Jesus to return.

Jesus knew the enormous personal risk in returning, but he committed himself to going anyway. So did someone else. The account is gripping:

> Then [Jesus] said to his disciples, "Let us go back to Judea."
>
> "But Rabbi," they said, "a short while ago the Jews tried to stone you, and yet you are going back there?" . . .
>
> "Let us go to [Lazarus]."
>
> Then Thomas . . . said to the rest of the disciples, "Let us also go, that we may die with him." (John 11:7-8, 15-16)

Thomas was committed to Jesus—perhaps more so than many of the other disciples. Yet he wasn't afraid to let people—even Jesus—know he had doubts. Thomas elicited some of the most famous words Jesus ever spoke.

> Thomas said to [Jesus], "Lord, . . . how can we know the way?"
>
> Jesus answered, "I am the way and the truth and the life. No one comes to the Father except through me. If you really knew me, you would know my Father as well.

From now on, you do know him and have seen him. . . . Anyone who has seen me has seen the Father." (John 14:5-7, 9)

From all indications, this was enough for Thomas—at least for a season. Like many of us, however, Thomas experienced something on his spiritual journey that rocked his world, bringing latent doubts to the surface. For some of us, those moments come in times of pain and suffering. For others, they flow from dysfunctional Christian community. For Thomas, it was the crucifixion of the One who claimed to be God in human form.

It was just too much.

Jesus had told Thomas and the other disciples that he had come to give his life away. In no uncertain terms, Jesus had informed them all that he was going to lay down his life for the sins of the world but that he would then come back from the dead.

Such an idea confounded their reasoning. As a result, when Jesus was crucified, Thomas was devastated. It was as if everything he had brought himself to believe, everything he had managed to trust, was ripped out from beneath him.

You cannot help but feel sorry for him.

What happened next should come as no surprise. Three days after his crucifixion, Jesus presented himself to some of the disciples—resurrected from the dead.

Now Thomas . . . was not with the disciples when Jesus

came. So the other disciples told him, "We have seen the Lord!"

But he said to them, "Unless I see the nail marks in his hands and put my finger where the nails were, and put my hand into his side, I will not believe it." (John 20:24-25)

This wasn't a belligerent skeptic; this was someone distraught, in pain from mental confusion. In essence, he said, "I can't go there with you. I just can't buy it—not now. The only way I could even imagine opening up my mind again is if I see him with my own eyes and touch him with my own hands."

People throughout history have looked down on Thomas for this crisis of faith. Jesus, however, did not.

A week later his disciples were in the house again, and Thomas was with them. Though the doors were locked, Jesus came and stood among them and said, "Peace be with you!" Then he said to Thomas, "Put your finger here; see my hands. Reach out your hand and put it into my side. Stop doubting and believe."

Thomas said to him, "My Lord and my God!" (John 20:26-28)

Jesus appears again and turns *immediately* to Thomas. Rather than to condemn, the appearance was designed to deal directly with his doubt. To paraphrase Jesus' words, "Put your finger in, touch my hand, put your hand in my side.

And when you are done, put aside any doubt as to who and what is spiritually real for your life. I want you to see that what I told you is true. I am who I said: the way and the truth and the life."

And Thomas believed.

We might be tempted to think, *If Jesus showed up from the dead, I'd say "My Lord and my God" too!* Scott Stapp, lead singer for the musical group Creed, would be among those with such sentiments. Raised in a Christian home, as a teenager he constantly asked God to prove himself. He'd lie in bed and say, "God, if you're real, just make my light go off so I won't doubt it."[15]

Apparently God didn't.

But Jesus said something intriguing to Thomas: "Because you have seen me, you have believed; blessed are those who have not seen and yet have believed" (John 20:29). This verse leads many people to view Thomas' doubt in a negative light, yet it is less a word to Thomas, perhaps, than to the nature of meaningful faith. God could inspire the most rationally conclusive argument for his existence; he could appear in all of his glory and stun the world into spontaneous worship. But God seeks relationships with free people who choose to bow before him in uncoerced love and devotion.

Many people *have* had experiences of God's "appearance"—times when indisputable evidence of the reality of God was granted to their fragile and developing faith. For some, it was through an overwhelming sense of God's presence at a key moment in life. For others, it was during an event that could only be called supernatural or miraculous. In many cases a deep awareness of the truth of Scripture or the gospel seemed to present itself to people's minds. In a way, Jesus *has* come and showed his nail-pierced hands to our skeptical intellects, and we too have said, "My Lord and my God!"

THIS STORY IS TRUE

On the wall of my study is an enlarged photograph I took of Addison's Walk, just behind Magdalen College in Oxford, England. The path runs beside several streams of the River Cherwell. During a summer of study I took evening walks there on a regular basis. It became very dear to me, though I was not the first to hold it prized.

On Saturday, September 19, 1931, C. S. Lewis invited two friends to dine with him in his rooms on Staircase III of New Building at Magdalen, where he taught. One was Hugo Dyson, a lecturer in English literature at Reading University. The other was J. R. R. Tolkien, author of *The Hobbit* and *The Lord of the Rings*. After they had dined, Lewis took his guests on a walk through the Magdalen grounds, ending with a stroll down Addison's Walk. There they began to discuss metaphor and myth.

Lewis had long appreciated myth. As a boy he loved the great Norse stories of the dying god Balder, and as a man he grew to respect the power of myth throughout the history of language and literature. But he didn't *believe* in them. Beauti-

ful and moving though they might be, they were, he concluded, ultimately untrue. As he expressed to Tolkien, myths
are "lies and therefore worthless, even though breathed
through silver."

"No," said Tolkien. "They are not lies."

Later Lewis recalled that at the moment Tolkien uttered
those words, "a rush of wind . . . came so suddenly on the
still, warm evening and sent so many leaves pattering down
that we thought it was raining. We held our breath."

Tolkien's point was that within myths were something of
eternal truth. They talked on, and Lewis became convinced
by the force of Tolkien's argument. They returned to Lewis's
rooms, where the conversation turned toward Christianity.
Here, Tolkien argued, the poet who invented the story was
none other than God himself, and the images he used were
real men and women—actual history.

Lewis was floored.

"Do you mean," he asked, "that the death and resurrection
of Christ is the old 'dying God' story all over again?"

Yes, Tolkien answered, except that here is a *real* dying God,
with a precise location in history and definite historical consequences. The old myth has become fact. Such joining of
faith and intellect had never occurred to Lewis.

It was now 3 a.m., and Tolkien had to go home. Lewis and
Dyson escorted him down the stairs, crossed the quadrangle
and let him out by a little postern gate on Magdalen Bridge.
Lewis remembered that "Dyson and I found more to say to

one another, strolling up and down the cloister of New Building, so that we did not get to bed till 4."

Twelve days later Lewis wrote to his close boyhood friend Arthur Greeves: "I have just passed on from believing in God to definitely believing in Christ—in Christianity. I will try to explain this another time. My long night talk with Dyson and Tolkien had a good deal to do with it."[16]

The great call of the Christian faith is not to eliminate doubt but to believe within the dynamic of doubt. Not all that lies beyond our mind's capacity to understand is myth. Indeed, it may point to the deepest of realities. For the final leg of faith's journey involves the intellect being "certain of what we do not see" (Hebrews 11:1).

Six

THE MYSTERY OF GOD

Admire and adore the Author of the telescopic universe, love
and esteem the work, do all in your power to lessen ill, and
increase good, but never assume to comprehend.
·   JOHN ADAMS

Summer just isn't summer in the Carolinas without a trip to
hear fellow North Carolinian James Taylor in concert at an
outdoor amphitheater. His song "That's Why I'm Here" teases
people who make these annual pilgrimages with their "baby,
. . . blanket . . . and bucket of beer" to hear "*Fire and Rain*
again and again and again."

People like me.

After one of his annual shows in Charlotte, Taylor was interviewed on the subject of spirituality. With great candor,
Taylor revealed that for him "God has not always been an answer, but the name of a question." Going further, Taylor
noted that what is "particularly important" is "what we do
with the mystery."[1]

We are filled with questions that seem to have no answers.

Fair, honest questions about dinosaurs and evolution, black holes and quantum physics, miracles and angels, dreams and déjà vu. Then there are the mysteries about God that play with your mind. How can a Being have no beginning? No creation, no start—just always there. There are things that we want to have explained, and God seems to keep us in the dark.

Whereas doubt is the struggle with what God has revealed for us to believe, mystery is the struggle with what he has kept hidden. When it comes to books, movies or plays, we like mysteries, *but only because they're solved.* An Agatha Christie or P. D. James tale that never told us who committed the crime would be unbearable.

Father Daniel Lanahan, director of a Franciscan ministry, notes that the more he studies and reflects and prays, the more incomprehensible God becomes. "When I was a student studying for a degree in theology, I actually spoke as if I knew a lot about God and about the ways of the Divine. . . . Today I am more aware of being an 'agnostic.' The Holy Unknowable is my God; I believe firmly in the unfathomable mystery of God."[2]

The irony of spiritual development is that the more you journey in faith, the less convinced you become of all that you can know.

MYSTERY IS TO BE EXPECTED

Disconcerting though it may be, when it comes to God, we must expect mystery. The great prophet Isaiah records these words from God himself:

> My thoughts are not your thoughts,
>   neither are your ways my ways. . . .
> As the heavens are higher than the earth,
>   so are my ways higher than your ways
>   and my thoughts than your thoughts. (Isaiah 55:8-9)

God is infinite, and we are finite. He is eternal and all-powerful and all-knowing; we are not. If an exhaustive understanding of God were possible, then God would cease to be God, for if our minds could fathom all of the mysteries of God, then God would be no greater than our minds.

A mystery is not the same as a verbal puzzle, where core concepts are accessible but must be rightly understood. When the Bible maintains, for example, that we must die in order to live, the apparent tension dissolves with the understanding that it refers not to physical death but to death to a sinful spirit.

Mystery is also distinct from agnosticism, where two contradictory ideas are given equal weight in the belief that evidence will eventually reveal one idea to be superior to the other.

Mystery stands apart from paradox as well, which is simply a contradiction accepted as truth. A "round square" would be a paradox.[3]

A mystery is beyond rational explanation. It is not inherently self-contradictory; we just lack the ability to penetrate what an anonymous fourteenth-century spiritual writer called "the cloud of unknowing" that encircles it.

And there is a cloud. Consider God's swift response to Job, who dared question the mysteries surrounding God's actions as if the veil between humanity and God should not exist.

"Where were you when I laid the earth's foundation?
 Tell me, if you understand.
Who marked off its dimensions? . . .

Have you ever given orders to the morning,
 or shown the dawn its place? . . .

Have you journeyed to the springs of the sea
 or walked in the recesses of the deep?
Have the gates of death been shown to you? . . .
Have you comprehended the vast expanses of the earth?
 Tell me, if you know all this. . . .

Surely you know. . . .
 You have lived so many years! . . .

Who endowed the heart with wisdom
 or gave understanding to the mind?" . . .

Then Job answered the LORD:

"I am unworthy—how can I reply to you?
 I put my hand over my mouth.
I spoke once, but I have no answer. . . . I will say no

more." (Job 38:4-5, 12, 16-18, 21, 36; 40:3-5)

Some of our questions by their very nature cannot be answered by God. As C. S. Lewis once posed, "All nonsense questions are unanswerable. . . . Probably half the questions we ask—half our great theological and metaphysical questions—are like that."[4]

Other questions must remain unanswered because there are things we are not *ready* to comprehend. Theologically we are in many ways still children, and we need the protection accorded to childhood.

This is difficult to accept, particularly as we often seem to wish the very idea of childhood away. We use words like *childish* and *immature* as insults. Yet childhood is a time when a person is appropriately sheltered from certain experiences and knowledge. Only as children grow into adulthood are such "adult secrets" revealed in ways that they can be assimilated psychologically and spiritually. Children *should* be naive. That is what childhood is for.

But preserving childhood for a child can mean keeping adult secrets shrouded in mystery.

Corrie ten Boom tells of an event that took place when she was no more than ten or eleven as she traveled with her father on the train from Amsterdam to Haarlem. She stumbled upon a poem that had the word *sexsin* among its lines.

And so, seated next to Father in the train compartment, I suddenly asked, "Father, what is *sexsin?*"

He turned to look at me, as he always did when answering a question, but to my surprise he said nothing. At last he stood up, lifted his traveling case from the rack over our heads, and set it on the floor.

"Will you carry it off the train, Corrie?" he said.

I stood up and tugged at it. It was crammed with the watches and spare parts he had purchased that morning.

"It's too heavy," I said.

"Yes," he said. "And it would be a pretty poor father who would ask his little girl to carry such a load. It's the same way, Corrie, with knowledge. Some knowledge is too heavy for children. When you are older and stronger you can bear it. For now you must trust me to carry it for you."

And I was satisfied. More than satisfied—wonderfully at peace. There were answers to this and all my hard questions—for now I was content to leave them in my father's keeping.[5]

God is mysterious not simply because he is God but because we are children, and in his love our childhood is protected. We should view both our childhood and God's mysteries as a source of wonder and even comfort: there is a Creator, and we are among the created; there are answers to all things safely in our Father's keeping.

As we accept God's mysteries as little children, they become not so much frustrating as *alluring*.

MYSTERY REFLECTS OUR DEEPEST LONGINGS FOR GOD

While I might struggle with the mystery that surrounds God, deep down I want God to be more than I am, to know more than I do. I yearn for God to be beyond my understanding. As Vincent van Gogh said of his eventual rejection of his family's "whole system of religion": "That does not keep me from having a terrible need of—shall I say the word—religion. Then I go out at night to paint the stars." Kathleen Powers Erickson believes that his painting *Starry Night* reflects the "mystic's desire for union with the infinite God."[6]

We are all mystics. Rudolf Otto, in his classic work *The Idea of the Holy*, wrote that the *mysterium tremendum* (the totality of God's mystery—literally, "tremendous mystery") "is not simply something to be wondered at but something that entrances." In it and through it we feel "something that captivates and transports" us with a "strange ravishment" to the point of "dizzy intoxication."[7] Spirituality, in virtually every form, taps into our longing for the mysterious, our hunger for that which is not of this world.

"My religion could not be fiction, but it had to transcend facts."
BONO

Perhaps this hunger helps to explain why Christians, particularly Roman Catholics, have recited the rosary for centuries. Developed in parallel with the monastic tradition, the rosary's cycle of prayer outlines the history of salvation in light of its mystery. The repetition of prayers and the handling of beads are meant to create a space that allows the Holy Spirit to whisper, "Glory be to the Father."

The rosary begins with the blessing of the cross and the Apostles' Creed. On the first bead, the Lord's prayer is said. The next three beads call for "Hail Marys," a prayer made up of blessings on Mary by the angel Gabriel and her cousin Elizabeth (Luke 1:28, 42), and a fifteenth-century appeal to prayer for sinners. These are followed by a traditional doxology known commonly by the title "Glory Be to the Father." The heart of the rosary's cycle is found in three groups of "mysteries," each highlighting an aspect of the gospel: joyful mysteries such as the annunication, the birth of Christ and the presentation of Jesus at the temple; sorrowful mysteries such as the agony in the Garden of Gethsemane, the crown of thorns, and the carrying of the cross; and glorious mysteries such as the resurrection, the ascension and the coming of the Holy Spirit. Mystery is celebrated throughout the rosary; divine mysteries are understood as moving the praying heart toward faith.[8]

Mystery also influenced the design of the great Gothic cathedrals of the medieval era. Even to this day few step inside such buildings without experiencing some sensation of the holy. As a result, Gothic cathedrals made Christianity both attractive and compelling in the medieval era. While the mystery surrounding God is often unsettling, it is also attractive: we want to touch what is truly transcendent and experience what is authentically supernatural.

The prophet Isaiah came face to face with this mystery in all of its puzzlement and glory.

> I saw the Lord seated on a throne, high and exalted, and the train of his robe filled the temple. Above him were seraphs, each with six wings: With two wings they covered their faces, with two they covered their feet, and with two they were flying. And they were calling to one another:
> "Holy, holy, holy is the LORD Almighty;
>   the whole earth is full of his glory."
> At the sound of their voices the doorposts and thresholds shook and the temple was filled with smoke. (Isaiah 6:1-4)

In the Hebrew language, repeated words conveyed something of great significance. Here is more than the foundation for a future hymn. The strongest statement possible about God's character was being made. Indeed, this is the only occurrence in the Bible of an attribute of God being repeated three times. God is holy, *holy, holy!*

Holiness is more than purity or sinlessness. To be holy is, at its heart, to be "set apart," "wholly different." Holiness is, by its very nature, *mysterious*. God's mysterious holiness made Isaiah cower.

> Woe to me! . . . I am ruined! For I am a man of unclean lips, and I live among a people of unclean lips, and my eyes have seen the King, the LORD Almighty. (Isaiah 6:5)

God's holiness makes us cower as well. Isn't the root of terror an encounter with that which is not like us? As a child I listened late at night to *CBS Radio Mystery Theater,* hosted by E. G. Marshall, thrilled by the unsettling entrance into the world of the supernatural it provided. When Isaiah encountered the holy God in all his mystery and wonder, he had a similar rush of adrenaline. It scared him. It wasn't comfortable. But another emotion surged in him: attraction. Isaiah wanted to be a part of this mystery, to connect his life with its inscrutable, enigmatic nature. And then God reached out to him.

> Then one of the seraphs flew to me with a live coal in his hand, which he had taken with tongs from the altar. With it he touched my mouth and said, "See, this has touched your lips; your guilt is taken away and your sin atoned for."
>
> Then I heard the voice of the Lord saying, "Whom shall I send? And who will go for us?"
>
> And I said, "Here am I. Send me!" (Isaiah 6:6-8)

"In the face of an overpowering mystery, you don't dare disobey."

ANTOINE DE SAINT-EXUPERY, *THE LITTLE PRINCE*

Here was God unfiltered, raw—the way a deep part of us wants him. Isaiah wanted nothing more than to order his life around this awe-inspiring God.

While we may struggle with God's mystery, we are also drawn to it. Our motivation to seek God flows from love coupled with a deep sense of awe; the awe is natural, indispensable.

Consider what faith would be like without it. As doubt can lead to faith, mystery can—and should—lead to awe.

IT'S NOT ALL MYSTERY

But God does not want to be wholly mysterious to us. If anything, human history is the story of God making himself known to us.

God spoke through Moses to the Pharaoh and the Israelites. He spoke to humankind through prophets and supernatural activities. He inspired the writings contained in the Bible. And ultimately, he came to earth. We worship a Mystery that can also be *known*. Thus God has given us both mystery and revelation.

If you want to connect with a horse, the best way is to become a horse. If you want to make sense of yourself to an ant, the most effective way is to become an ant. God wanted to make himself known to us, so God became a human being in the Person of Jesus. Through Jesus, God revealed what he is like and how we can be in relationship with him,

> that [we] may have the full riches of complete understanding, in order that [we] may know the mystery of God, namely, Christ, in whom are hidden all the treasures of wisdom and knowledge. (Colossians 2:2-3)

PART FOUR

The Struggle of Our Strength

To love God with our strength is to love God with our actions. This is the aspect of loving God we are most comfortable with—at least in theory—for it's very much the way we tend to *think* about loving. Whether it's buying a dozen roses, bestowing a kiss, or lending a helping hand, we act out of feelings of love. If demonstrations of "strength" are not present, then love itself is often suspect.

Yet love calls for humility, and it is far too easy to consider certain acts beneath us. Love calls for sacrifice, and we tend to give of our strength only from a sense of surplus. More than anything, love calls for submission—committing ourselves to do what love requires or requests—and we don't like to submit.

In reality, love is selfless but we are selfish; love is giving but we are demanding; love thinks of others but we think mostly of ourselves. The apostle Paul gives a sane, authentic rendering of the actual state of affairs: "I do not understand what I do. For what I want to do I do not do, but what I hate I do" (Romans 7:15).

This is the struggle of loving God with all of our strength: accepting and obeying the call of love.

And obedience does not come easily.

Seven

THE WILL OF GOD

*Nor is it to be wondered, that the will of God, when clothed
in words, should be liable to that doubt and uncertainty
which unavoidably attends that sort of conveyance.*
JOHN LOCKE
CONCERNING HUMAN UNDERSTANDING 3.9.23

I have spent my entire life in pursuit of independence. As a
young boy I changed my "given" name from Emery to Jim.
My parents were aghast, but I was determined to be called
what I wanted to be called. When I was a teenager, I dreamed
of getting out from underneath the control of my parents and
the confines of our home—to come home when I wanted and
to buy what I chose. In college, I couldn't wait to escape the
rules of the dormitory, the demands of my professors and the
regimen of the academic program. I entered the workforce
dreaming of financial independence so that I would not have
to answer to a supervisor or corporate culture. Stage after
stage, era after era, the goal was the same: freedom from answering to others.

And when I came to God, what did I hear?

"Do what I say."

People experience deeply emotional conversions to the Christian faith, begin great journeys of spiritual growth, and embrace a vigorously Christian worldview, but at the first sign of a call to obedience—even as simple an act as baptism—all bets are off.

Baptism, established by Jesus as a rite of initiation, marks our entrance into the Christian community. As a symbol, it reflects the washing away of our sins as we enter into Christ's death, burial and resurrection. But the significance of baptism goes beyond its symbolic role. In a sense, right at the beginning of our relationship with him, Jesus establishes a litmus test to see whether our will—our strength—is subjected to his.

And that is, contrary to popular opinion, the real issue.

NOT ABOUT KNOWLEDGE

When we exclaim, "If only I knew what God wanted me to do, I would do it!" we are not often serious. Books on finding the will of God are legion, but the struggle is following God's will, not knowing it. We already know far more of what is required of us than we could ever begin to act upon. The moral will of God is the most widely known aspect of the Christian faith. Perhaps we do not wish to be moral.

Or are we just not *able* to be moral? Our moral lives would be much easier if we could say with theological conviction,

"I couldn't help myself." There is a thin line between the inevitability of sin in our lives (which we *can* say with theological conviction), and a fatalism that dismisses failure with a wink of the eye.

One of the greatest theological debates in Christian history involved this distinction. Pelagius, a moralist living in the fourth and fifth centuries A.D., was deeply concerned that people live good and ethical lives. He saw the concepts of total depravity (the inherent corruption of fallen humanity) and the inevitability of sin as counterproductive. How can telling people that they cannot help but sin encourage a moral life? So Pelagius emphasized that we do not enter the world biased toward evil and that we have the ability and freedom to choose the good and moral life. Following his thought to its logical end, Pelagius taught that humans could merit salvation on their own by perfectly fulfilling God's commands without sinning.

While agreeing with Pelagius that the image of God in human beings was not entirely lost in the Fall of Adam and Eve, Augustine, a bishop in the church and contemporary of Pelagius, maintained that we *had* lost the ability *not* to sin. Augustine saw the history of the human will in three stages, which he gave succinct Latin titles.

- Before the Fall we were *posse non peccari et mori* (able not to sin and die). This was the age of innocence.

- After the Fall, we found ourselves *non posse non peccari et*

115

mori (not able not to sin and die). This is the age of responsibility.

- Yet one day we will be in heaven, where we will be *non posse peccari et mori* (not able to sin and die). This will be the age of fulfillment.

One of Augustine's famous analogies was that of a set of balances, or scales, representing good and evil. If the scales were properly balanced, someone could weigh the merits in doing good against those in doing evil, and make a choice. But as a result of the Fall of humanity passed on through Adam, though the scales work, they are seriously out of balance. Human beings are now prone to wrongdoing.

The teachings of Pelagius were condemned as heretical by the Council of Ephesus in 431. Yet though he was discounted, Pelagius forced thinkers such as Augustine (and through them the church) to sharpen their understanding of the tension between our orientation toward sin and our call to obey the will of God.

Augustine sympathized with Pelagius's concern for the struggle to obey the will of God, but he had long seen *grace* as the liberating force that would set the human will free from its bondage to sin. Grace tips the scales back and allows a person to choose that which is moral and good. Augustine thus maintained that grace is *prevenient*—it "goes ahead of," or comes before our conversion and sanctification, preparing in us a will to choose good. Grace is also *operative*—it "operates" on us for the purpose of salvation, independent of anything we do. Finally and most important here, it is *cooperative*—once we become Christians, we are able to cooperate with grace to grow in holiness.

That is, if we *want* to cooperate.

In reality we are pulled between our inherently sinful nature and our capacity to pursue the will of God through cooperative grace. "When I get honest, I admit I am a bundle of paradoxes," writes Brennan Manning.

> I believe and I doubt, I hope and get discouraged, I love and I hate, I feel bad about feeling good, I feel guilty about not feeling guilty. I am trusting and suspicious. I am honest and I still play games. Aristotle said I am a rational animal; I say I am an angel with an incredible capacity for beer.[1]

And so are we all.

THE TWO WILLS OF GOD

So we are free and able to pursue and obey the will of God. But is God free? Is God able to allow his will not to happen? If so, what does this mean for our struggle to follow him?

There are actually two senses of the "will" of God. What might be called God's *wishes* is his general intention—the values with which he is pleased. We have great freedom under this sense of God's will; there is much we can do that goes *against* his wishes. For example, we can choose to sin against him, to which God responds, "So be it," though our sins are abhorrent to him. His willingness to endure our rejection of his will allows us to freely choose to do his will, and to experience his great pleasure.

The more formal sense of God's "will" is better deemed God's *specific* intentions, what he has decided will actually occur. Human beings are incapable of thwarting God's specific intentions.

The struggle of human will plays out in the tension between our freedom and God's wishes. Whenever the New Testament makes mention of our responsibility in light of God's will, the Greek word used is *thelema*, which expresses God's wishes or desires, not his resolute intentions. God's wishes or desires demand our cooperation for their fulfillment.[2]

But we don't always want to cooperate. We resist, rationalize and, all too often, reject him. We water down, ignore or argue with what he's said. We find people who will contend that he never said it or that it no longer applies to our day.

But *why*? Beyond our sin, why is following Christ such a challenge to Christ-followers? I have become aware of at least two reasons: we confuse our self-oriented fulfillment (and the steps involved in pursuing it) with God's will, and we do not think God knows what is best for us.

FORTY

On my fortieth birthday, my staff threw a surprise birthday wake. They dressed in black, decorated the location in black (even down to black balloons) and presented me with a cake designed as a tombstone. On the gray icing was written (in black, of course), "Here lies the youth of James Emery White."

Truth be told, my fortieth birthday did hold something of a death for me. I had spent my twenties and thirties in pursuit of goal-oriented accomplishments. As I approached forty, I knew I was entering a new season of life, and I set out to discover what I was to do with the rest of my life.

Instead of a discovery, I had a rude awakening.

As I began to explore questions such as "What do I do best?" and "Where could I make the most impact?" I found the Holy Spirit whispering into my thoughts, "These are the wrong questions." Puzzled, and more than a bit disconcerted, I began to pray and reflect on what was wrong with my quest.

It dawned on me that in all of Scripture, not one person went on a journey of self-discovery in order to find and follow God's will. I had bought into the self-absorbed assumption that what mattered was "who I am in Christ," which often operates as a euphemism for personal fulfillment and satisfaction.

I found that people in Scripture were *invited* to do something (as with Jeremiah and the disciples), *selected* to do something (David and Samuel, for example), or presented with the *opportunity* to do something (as were Esther and Deborah). I could not find a single case of someone going off in search of their identity, much less ordering their steps to fulfill who they were made to be (outside of their identity as a child of God). Not once did someone in Scripture say, "This would satisfy me/make me happy/allow me to be healthy and whole." They simply lived their lives, and *when* God brought something their way, the faithful did it.

I don't write this to dismiss the importance of finding and using our spiritual gifts or "doing what you are." But the evidence from Scripture ought to temper much of our current fascination with making self-discovery and fulfillment the end-all of God's will for our life. Instead the relational dimension of the spiritual journey, and *calling* in its deepest and most profound sense, ought to be our ultimate pursuit. "Calling," writes Os Guinness,

> is the truth that God calls us to himself so decisively that everything we are, everything we do, and everything we have is invested with a special devotion and dynamism lived out as a response to his summons and service.[3]

According to German philosopher Friedrich Nietzsche, one of the few individuals bold enough to challenge the morality of Christianity, we have only two choices in how our lives are played out: obey ourselves and follow our will to power, or be commanded by another. And who would rather be commanded?

To embrace a call requires a willingness to follow. And as Walter Brueggeman has observed, a "sense of call in our time is profoundly countercultural. . . . The ideology of our time is that we can live 'an uncalled life,' one not referred to any purpose beyond one's self."[4]

When personal fulfillment is allowed to take the place of calling, our lives become little more than exercises in self-indulgence. Ironically, we were created such that our deepest fulfillment is found *as* we submit to God's calling on our life. The reason is simple: we are called first and foremost to Someone, not to something or to somewhere.

TRUSTING GOD'S LEAD

Confusing personal fulfillment with God's will is only the surface issue in the struggle of our wills. The critical concern is trust, which goes against the grain of our self-protective, self-determining nature.

No one wants to come out and say that they do not trust God's leadership. Yet we often don't, for to do so involves giving up control, and we do not want to give up control to *anyone*.

Still, we often must sacrifice self-determination to gain competent direction. When I board a plane, I gladly surrender control to the pilots. I have no desire to enter the cockpit because I know that they are better suited to guide and direct the aircraft. Have I lost anything by surrendering control to them? No, I simply gain the benefit of their competence.

When it comes to life, we insist on seeing ourselves as pilots. We forget that we haven't logged in many hours in flight training.

The Bible offers wise counsel at the heart of our struggle:

Trust in the LORD with all your heart
   and lean not on your own understanding;
in all your ways acknowledge him,
   and he will make your paths straight.
   (Proverbs 3:5-6)

The author knew that we struggle to trust in God over against our *own* understanding, to acknowledge God in all of *our* ways. We follow God's will only after we have discovered anew a fresh dissatisfaction with our self-leadership and a fresh appreciation of God's competence to lead us.

Barbara Tuchman, twice winner of the Pulitzer Prize for history, studied the tendency of governments to pursue policies contrary to their own interests. From Montezuma's surrender of his empire to Japan's attack on Pearl Harbor, governments have undertaken many a "march of folly" marked by self-destructive decisions in the face of known and compelling alternatives.[5]

We must come to understand self-leadership as life's great "march of folly." This must be the decisive act of our wills in the face of God's will: trust in God, or face ruin.

But even once we've recognized the difference between our will and God's will, and the advantages of God's leadership over self-leadership, we face a struggle in our will. In the end we must make our choice.

THE GREAT DRAMA

Jesus found his perfect obedience to the will of God tested in the Garden of Gethsemane. Jesus did not want to go to the cross. He begged the Father for another way to reconcile humanity to God. Scripture speaks of Jesus sweating blood, a medical condition known as hematidrosis, associated with only the most severe cases of psychological stress.

Jesus was fully God *and* fully human, and no human ever has been asked, or ever will be asked, to do what Jesus was asked by God to do. Jesus faced not simply death but an agonizing death that included taking the sin of all humanity on himself. At the moment of His death, Jesus would carry the weight of the sins of the world.

- Every rape, every murder, every lie, every betrayal, every adulterous relationship, every act of child abuse.

- Every addiction, every image from the sordid world of pornography, every rattle of slavery's chains.

- The hunger pangs from every famine, the shudder from every winter chill from homelessness.

- The evils of terrorism and genocide, war and oppression.

Jesus would carry their stain. He would *be* that sin.

But that wasn't the end of it. At the moment of his death, for the first and only time in all of eternity, Jesus would lose fellowship with the Father. The community of the Trinity would be shattered, and Jesus would be left utterly, terribly alone.

No wonder he sweat drops of blood.

God was always willing for Jesus to die in the place of others. Of course, Jesus pleaded for another way to achieve the ends of the love he shared with his Father for the world. But after a night of heart-wrenching prayer confirmed the desire of the Father's heart, Jesus accepted every aspect of its path. He submitted himself to the cross with the struggle settled: "Not my will, but yours be done" (Luke 22:42).

Jesus embraced what I must accept: God's calling as sovereign over my personal desires and sense of satisfaction, and radical trust in God's leadership.

In other words, I have a choice that can, and must, be chosen.

Eight

THE DECEPTION OF GOD

Is a dream a lie if it don't come true,
or is it something worse?
BRUCE SPRINGSTEEN, "THE RIVER"

For three years a top executive scientist was employed at Becton Dickinson, one of the nation's largest medical technology companies, where he supervised the development of numerous new supplies, devices and systems for use by healthcare professionals, medical research institutions, industry and the general public. His résumé was impressive: medical degree, law degree, Ph.D. in microbiology; the list of scientific papers he had written alone covered several pages. Past employment included a high-ranking AIDS research position at Abbot Laboratories, one of the largest pharmaceutical companies in the world.

But the scientist had kept some secrets from his employer, his publisher, the professional society he had joined and the publicly traded company that had appointed him to its board. He had been sent to prison and had his medical license revoked for trying to murder his wife by smothering her with a plastic-encased pillow. On one résumé he listed his "business address" as P.O. Box 1200, Dixon, Illinois, without mentioning that this was the address for inmate mail at the Dixon Correctional Facility. He was fired soon after executives learned of his past and the pattern of lies and misrepresentations during a routine check of his credentials.

Becton Dickinson is not alone in feeling the sting of deception. That same summer Sunbeam Corporation discovered that a former top executive had been fired by two other companies and had concealed the information from Sunbeam. In spring 2001 Lucent Technologies discovered that its director of recruiting had previously pled guilty to five felony charges, including forgery and grand theft. Camilla Jenkins, director of corporate communications at Beckton Dickinson, spoke on behalf of all the companies to assure concerned consumers that "there was no public impact or harm done."[1]

She may be right. But one can only imagine the *personal* harm done—the pain of colleagues who had risked friendship and intimacy only to be violated and betrayed.

In working as a pastor with couples whose marriages have been decimated by marital unfaithfulness, I have found that more destructive than the act itself is the dishonesty involved. Acts of deception woo their victims into a web of false reality, where they find themselves trapped by betrayals of trust. And some feel that not only their deceiver but God himself has perpetrated fraud against them, particularly as they strive to love God with all of their strength.

Jeremiah, who reluctantly accepted a call by God to be a prophet while still young enough to confess a lack of experience and maturity, was assured that he would be given the words to speak and the guidance needed for his calling. He was even promised protection and deliverance in the face of opposition (Jeremiah 1:7-8, 18-19). Yet Jeremiah served during one of the most tumultuous times in Israel's history and ultimately witnessed its destruction and captivity. Through a succession of kings and conquests, invasions and dispersions, Jeremiah faithfully proclaimed the word of God—and suffered greatly for it.

Jeremiah was ridiculed for predictions that did not quickly come to pass. The wicked he spoke out against seemed to prosper, and his antagonists flourished. He became the object of hostility and scorn, particularly in his hometown, where even his closest relatives plotted against him. He was beaten, arrested, cast into a cistern, even forced into exile. Tradition holds that he was stoned to death by his fellow Jews.

One can sympathize with Jeremiah's struggle with God: "O LORD, you deceived me, and I was deceived; / you overpowered me and prevailed" (Jeremiah 20:7). The Hebrew word translated *deceived* literally reads *seduced*. God had called Jeremiah to a task, and Jeremiah had answered "Yes" to God's summons with all of his strength, plunging himself into the work. And to what result?

The book of Lamentations in the Western Bible, written by

Jeremiah, is known among Hebrew-speaking people by its opening word, "How?" *('eka)*. That word sets the tone for five chapters of poetry marked by the shock and despair Jeremiah experienced during the destruction of Jerusalem and the humiliation of Judah. "Jeremiah makes it clear," observes Kathleen Norris, "that no one chooses to fall into the hands of such a God." Yet for all your bitter raging, "finally, you succumb to the God who has given you your identity in the first place."[2]

But what of this God?

Countless numbers of Christians have pursued faithfulness to God with all of their strength and found themselves seemingly punished for their fidelity or unrewarded for their virtue. They never realize the blessed life they thought that God promised them. They may resign themselves to continuing faithfulness to God, but they cannot help but feel deceived.

WHAT HAS GOD REALLY PROMISED?

There is a chasm between our expectations of life in relationship with God and what God has actually promised, particularly between God's definition of a blessed life and ours.

When we are candid, we admit that we expect from God a certain degree of direct provision when it comes to health, money and success. We may be theologically sophisticated enough to reject a "gospel of prosperity," but we still shun sin more to avoid punishment or curry favor than out of a pursuit of virtue. We are called to tithe out of appreciation and worship, but more often we tithe because we read in Malachi 3:10 of a promise that we'll receive even more (more money, we presume). Even the most basic spiritual disciplines are all too often motivated by a desire for personal spiritual fulfillment rather than a hunger for intimacy with the living God. We expect direct, tangible, earthly dividends for our investment in following God. Hence the enormous popularity of books both crass and sophisticated that offer keys to successful living, or praying, for God's favor.

"We naturally and wrongly assume we're here to experience something God has never promised," Christian psychologist Larry Crabb writes. When the one we depend on to give us a good life doesn't deliver, "we feel betrayed, let down, [and] thoroughly disillusioned."[3] Is God baiting us with our expectations, only to hook us into a life of disappointment?

To ask for God's blessing, according to the Bible, is to cry out for the incredible, wonderful goodness that only God has the power to give—not to beg God for what we could provide for ourselves. Biblical characters who sought God's blessing tended to leave the *details* up to God, so that God's blessing often translated into increased influence, responsibility and opportunity to make him known.

Can God's blessing include increased wealth or success? Of course, but that is not its *drive*. The now-famous biblical character Jabez prayed that his territory would be expanded (and seemingly received his wish) so that he could use his greater resources for *God*—not for his own sense of well-being, ego, fame or satisfaction. The motivation for Jabez was to *be* more, and to *do* more, for God, and God seems to have given it to him. God's blessing operates as easily through poverty as through prosperity, as evidenced by the lives of Francis of Assisi and Mother Teresa. God's plan for our lives may not include material gain, physical health, relational joy, vocational success and personal fulfillment. It does include character development, soul formation and investment in God's kingdom.

Some Christ-followers have learned to embrace this perspective.

David Ireland, diagnosed with a crippling neurological disease that would eventually take his life, was frequently asked, "Do you believe God will heal you?" He would respond with a question of his own: "Do I really need to be healed?" In his book, *Letters to an Unborn Child*, Ireland explained his thinking:

> I'm firmly convinced that God is extremely good and that He does love and understand all the world and all the people in it. Does He want to heal me? I can't even answer that. My faith is in the genuineness of God, not in whether He will do this or that to demonstrate His goodness. . . . That's not the nature of my relationship to God.[4]

Similarly, a young mother who had lost one child and was set to lose a second to a ravaging disease told the author of an article on "faith under torturous life conditions" that we are meant to engage the moral challenges brought to bear on our lives by God. Instead we come to God weakly, seeking comfort and remedy.[5] We seldom consider that God's blessing may very well be a life that withstands the crucible of a fallen world. And such a life, lived in light of the trustworthy character of God despite circumstances, stands favored above all.

THE FINAL WORD

The promise that was meant to fuel our strength was never a promise for this life. We were given a future hope: the promise of heaven. Unfortunately, heaven's stock has fallen in recent years. We have become blind to its vision and indifferent to its promise.

Jesus encouraged his followers that "no one who has left home or brothers or sisters or mother or father or children or fields for me and the gospel will fail to receive a hundred times as much in this present age . . . and in the age to come, eternal life" (Mark 10:29-30). We interpret Jesus' words through the lens of immediate material gain, but we seldom evaluate his promise and our lives in terms of an unfolding redemptive history. All that is "lost" in one world may well be regained a hundredfold in the new.

Wayne Ward, longtime professor of theology at The Southern Baptist Theological Seminary in Louisville, Kentucky, once told me of his first opportunity to preach. He was only a boy, but Dr. Benjamin Ware, pastor of the First

Baptist Church of Arkadelphia, Arkansas, invited him into his pulpit.

It was a difficult time for black Americans. The country was deeply segregated. If you were black, you couldn't drink from certain water fountains, eat at certain restaurants, use certain public bathrooms or even sit down in the front of a public bus. The parishioners of First Baptist Church sat slumped over, tired, discouraged, desperately in need of something to help them through the week.

Reverend Ware was in his eighties at the time, and one of the finest preachers and leaders of his day. Before the very Anglo Wayne, his knees knocking and his palms sweaty, approached the pulpit to speak, Dr. Ware addressed the congregation. "Before this young man comes to speak, I have some words to lift you up."

Though a highly educated man, Reverend Ware would often speak in ways that his people tended to speak. This day was no exception. The people lifted their heads a little, in expectation.

"I want tell you about Heab'n. Heab'n is a place where your hands ain't gonna hurt no more."

"Heab'n is a place where your feet ain't gonna hurt no more."

"Heab'n, why heab'n is a place where your back ain't gonna hurt no more."

Each line seemed to lift them up, give them hope. For their hands did hurt, their feet were swollen and their backs did ache from long hours of labor.

"Mary," he said, calling one of the members by name, "we buried your honey last week. Heab'n is a place where you'll hug him all day long."

Mary shook her head in affirmation, tears streaming down her face.

"Heab'n," Dr. Ware went on, "heab'n is a place where you ain't gonna cry no more."

Then he turned to Wayne and said, "Boy, you're loose, now go!"

And he *was* loose. And so were they.

Talk of heaven is not mere optimism. Indeed, mere optimism must be guarded *against*, for it is a pale imitation of faith and hope, which trust not that life will be good but that all things are in the hands of a particular, trustworthy Person. The "power of positive thinking" cannot be found in Scripture, whereas the trustworthiness of God and the promise of heaven are recurring themes in the Bible. Our faith is rooted in not the present but the future. It is based on not our single story but the wider narrative of the cosmic saga. When we misplace our faith, we ultimately find little to sustain it in the face of life's adversities. We are to live each day on its own terms, Christ tells us, as a safeguard against worry, but we are given advance knowledge of the final scene in God's saga as a safeguard against despair.

Admiral Jim Stockdale was the highest-ranking United States military officer in the "Hanoi Hilton" prison camp during the Vietnam War. Tortured over twenty times during his

eight-year imprisonment, Stockdale endured his time without any rights, a set release date or even the confidence that
he would see his family again. Yet he shouldered the burden
of command, willingly disfiguring himself with a razor to
prevent being used for propaganda, exchanging secret information with his wife through their letters, and instituting an
elaborate internal communications system between the fellow prisoners. After his release, he became the first three-star
officer in the history of the navy to wear both aviator wings
and the Congressional Medal of Honor.

How did Stockdale endure such torture, deprivation and
isolation without knowing the outcome? In a dialogue with
author Jim Collins, he simply said, "I never lost faith in the
end of the story. I never doubted not only that I would get
out, but also that I would prevail in the end and turn the experience into the defining event of my life, which, in retro-
spect, I would not trade."

"Who didn't make it out?" Collins asked.

"Oh, that's easy," he said.

The optimists . . . the ones who said "We're going to be
out by Christmas." And Christmas would come, and
Christmas would go. Then they'd say, "We're going to be
out by Easter." And Easter would come, and Easter
would go. And then Thanksgiving, and then it would be
Christmas again. And they died of a broken heart. . . .

This is a very important lesson. You must never confuse faith that you will prevail in the end—which you

can never afford to lose—with the discipline to confront the most brutal facts of your current reality, whatever they might be.[6]

The events of life that breed suspicion of God's deception should never be denied. Such feelings run deep and should be felt deeply, but there is a greater story of what loving God with all of our strength will produce: the story of redemptive history. God will have the final word when this world ends.

C. S. Lewis captures this future promise in the concluding words of his seven-volume *Chronicles of Narnia*.

> The things that began to happen . . . were so great and beautiful that I cannot write them. And for us this is the end of all stories, and we can most truly say that they all lived happily ever after. But for them it was only the beginning of the real story. All their life in this world and all their adventures in Narnia had only been the cover and the title page: now at last they were beginning Chapter One of the Great Story which no one on earth. has read: which goes on forever: in which every chapter is better than the one before.[7]

It will be for us as well.

PART FIVE

The Struggle
with Our Neighbors

Jesus wanted us to know that the great vision of God for our life is directed not simply toward heaven but toward earth. You cannot love God apart from loving people, and you cannot love people apart from loving God.

Jesus broadened the interpretation of an instruction from the Old Testament—"Do not seek revenge or bear a grudge against one of your people, but love your neighbor as yourself. I am the LORD" (Leviticus 19:18)—to its widest sense possible. To Jesus, a neighbor was not simply someone among "your people"; Jesus counted among his, and our, neighbors the chance acquaintance, the stranger, the person on the street.

People resisted Jesus' radical idea. He was asked to clarify who specifically would be included in his definition of neighbor. Jesus responded with the tale of the Good Samaritan, which told of an act of love between two warring parties known for their deep-rooted hatred and mistrust.

Suddenly a radical teaching became scandalous. And it remains scandalous, for our Samaritan struggle continues when it comes to loving those who are dangerous or those we simply dislike.

Nine

THE DISLIKE OF PEOPLE

It is impossible you should hate a man from whom you have received no injury. By hatred, therefore, you mean no more than dislike, which is no sufficient objection against your marrying of him.
HENRY FIELDING, *TOM JONES* 7.3

Thanks to <www.justatip.com>, you can finally tell annoying people exactly what you think of them. Through this portal, you can send a free, anonymous e-mail to someone about whatever it is about them you do not like. Just click on a problem from a list including such classics as "bad date," "cheapskate," "fashion challenged," "bad breath" or even "dandruff." Answer a few questions, and <www.justatip.com> delivers the bad news.

The process isn't perfect. The site posts reactions (also without names), and sometimes people track down tipsters and exact revenge. "Five of my friends and I got together and sent one of our teachers a 'bad teacher tip,'" noted one disillusioned user. "The next day (she) gave us a pop quiz."[1]

The broad declaration of Jesus to "love your neighbor," as popularly perceived, is not difficult. We don't mind loving our neighbors as long as they're not *actual* neighbors who erect fences six inches on our side of the property line or coworkers competing with us for a promotion. We would much prefer the idea of loving neighbors in a *general* sense: strangers beset with misfortune who will accept a meal or an anonymous check. We want to love humanity in general, and we are willing to be "good Samaritans" in generic, faceless encounters.

Whereas in Jesus' day the command to love your neighbor had to be *extended* for its impact to avoid being muted, in our day it must be *narrowed.*

Disliking someone is taboo in our day, particularly for Christians. So we preface our list of criticisms with overtures of brotherly or sisterly love: "I love them, but . . ." or, in the South, "Bless her heart, she just . . ." If you can smile sweetly while you say it, it's even better. Several examples by an anonymous author came to me in an forwarded e-mail:

- "Bless his heart, if they put his brain on the head of a pin, it'd roll around like a BB on a six lane highway."

- "Bless her heart, she can't do a thing about those thighs of hers."

- "Even though they had that baby seven months after they got married, bless their hearts, it weighed ten pounds!"

But we live in community with people like these, and we are called to love them. Therein lies the struggle.

UNDERSTANDING THE REACTION

The complexities underlying relational chemistry have never been exhaustively explored. It doesn't help that most of us are dysfunctional relationally to begin with. One of the biggest problems monasteries face is that people come to them "having no sense of what it means to live communally. Schooled in individualism, often having families so disjointed that even meals in common were a rarity, they find it extremely difficult to adjust to monastic life."[2]

Our dislike of others may flow from their acts of cruelty toward us. Many of the people I dislike intensely have wounded me through betrayal, callous insensitivity or behind-the-back slander. The deeper the wound, the more hatred that boils up in me.

Or we may dislike others as an extension of our dislike of the situation in which we interact with them. A prostitute named Daisy told Alexa Albert that her profession made her feel "degraded, dehumanized, used, . . . ashamed, humiliated, embarrassed, insulted, . . . violated." She went on to describe her clients, many of whom felt intimately connected to her, with terms such as "pig, dog, animal, uncaring, user, slave owner, . . . mean, thoughtless, rude, crude, blind."[3]

Often our dislike of others reflects our own internal insecurities. We are threatened by those who have strengths where we are weak, or are accomplished where we have failed; our dislike of people flows from our dislike of ourselves. Psychotherapist Larry Crabb suggests that we believe that the deeper and most true things about ourselves are bad. He challenges us to see the good in people, including ourselves, buried beneath the pettiness and empire-building ambitions that irritate us so badly. Can we accept fellow Christians the way Christ accepts us, forgiving each other and believing there is something better? [4]

We think that we cannot, and so we are tempted to do nothing about our dislike of others.

If relationships become too uncomfortable, we disengage. We change jobs, move out of a neighborhood, find a new church or leave our marriage. We minimize relational life as portable and disposable. But the distaste for others will remain as long as we view them as nothing more than distasteful.

JESUS IN DISGUISE

An American visitor to Mother Teresa could not fathom her commitment to the outcasts on the streets in the slums of Calcutta. Her reply corrected his vision: "First we meditate on Jesus, . . . and then we go out and look for him in disguise." [5]

The people around us, even the ones we dislike, are sons and daughters of God. Our bond with them through our common creation, and shared love of the Creator, is immense. They are not simply "others" but fellow bearers of the image of God, and eternity is written on their souls. "You have never talked to a mere mortal," C. S. Lewis writes. "Nations, cultures, arts, civilisations—these are mortal, and their life is to ours as the life of a gnat. But it is immortals whom we joke with, work with, marry, snub, and exploit. . . . Next to the Blessed Sacrament itself, your neighbour is the holiest object presented to your senses."[6]

Such a perspective cannot, however, be gained by an act of the will. Our hearts must be purposefully directed toward a vision of God in others and nurtured under the warm rays of grace. A loving, Godlike gaze toward others is a directional choice within a life journey.

In his little book *The Power of the Powerless*, Christopher de Vinck writes of his brother, Oliver. Born blind, Oliver could neither see nor speak. His head was large, hands small, legs twisted. His feet were as tiny as a five-year-old's. Severe brain damage left him and his body in a permanent state of helplessness. He couldn't learn. He couldn't even lift his head. Oliver had to be spoon-fed and sponge-bathed, and someone had to change his diapers.

"I was suddenly overwhelmed with the realization that I loved all those people, that they were mine and I theirs, that we could not be alien to one another even though we were total strangers. It was like waking from a dream of separateness."

THOMAS MERTON,
CONJECTURES OF A
GUILTY BYSTANDER

Oliver's family loved him for thirty-two years.

Christopher, a high-school English teacher, told his students the story of his brother. As he described Oliver's lack of response, a boy in the last row raised his hand and said, "You mean he was a vegetable." As Christopher pondered the student's words, his mind traveled to the times he changed his brother's diapers, tickled his chest and made him laugh, and pulled the shades down on the window over the bed to keep the sun from burning Oliver's sensitive skin. Christopher said to the student, "Well, I guess you could call him a vegetable. I called him Oliver, my brother. You would have loved him."[7]

In the parable of the sheep and the goats (Matthew 25:31-46) we are reminded that lovingkindness to others is lovingkindness toward Christ. Mother Teresa seems to have followed this model in the cultivation of her own heart. "Because we cannot see Christ we cannot express our love to him; but our neighbours we can always see, and we can do to them what if we saw him we would like to do to Christ."[8]

But how does one love Jesus through those who are hard to love?

WHERE TO BEGIN

Jesus' most famous insight into healthy relational interaction, the "golden rule," has become so familiar to us that it seems trite. Yet treating others the way we would want to be treated helps us through the struggle of disliking others. The secret ingredient of the golden rule is grace.

We talk much of grace, but we tend to live by the letter of the law. Whereas grace involves freely giving forgiveness and forbearance when it is totally undeserved, our lives are gripped by justice—no forgiveness, no forbearance. Yet grace cannot remain in the realm of "ideas." It exists to be *applied*.

"Do not waste time bothering whether you 'love' your neighbour," C. S. Lewis wrote. "Act as if you did. . . . When you are behaving as if you loved someone, you will presently come to love him."[9]

So we act in grace in order to come to love. Yet how do we allow grace to override our dislikes?

GRACE APPLIED TO DIFFERENCES

Our default mode when it comes to others is simple: "You should be like me." We consider ourselves normal, the way people are supposed to be. We judge people by how we would act, how we would think, and how we would feel. So if people are not as we are, then there is something wrong with them.

Grace reminds us that people are different in every conceivable way.

There are extroverts who can't crowd enough interactions with others into their life, and introverts who would be utterly drained by even a single such weekend.

There are people who are naturally neat and organized: they make to-do lists, they could tell you their afternoon schedule for a week from Thursday, and at the end of the day they fold their underwear. Then there are those who fly by the seat of their pants: they run late everywhere they go, the couldn't tell you what they're doing tonight, and at the er the day they can't even *find* their underwear.

Left to ourselves, we would consider other peo in music, clothing or decorating just *wrong*. Bu accept that differences are a reality of community, and we celebrate the diversity of God's creation.

GRACE APPLIED TO WEAKNESS

Areas where a person struggles profoundly with key issues of life are not easy for others to take. Spend an afternoon on a playground, and you will quickly see that children naturally revile other children for being overweight, wearing braces, having some kind of physical deformity or wearing second-hand clothes, or for not being bright or pretty.

As we get older we no longer circle around at recess to taunt and tease others. Instead we whisper our comments to others or make snide remarks as they pass by. We size people up, form judgments and in the end condemn them for who they are—particularly when their weakness is in one of our areas of strength.

Someone who is good with money has little patience or tolerance toward someone who tends toward being a spendthrift. Someone who has been naturally thin their entire life 'arsh and insensitive toward someone who has struggobesity since childhood. We understand weakness rson only if we share the weakness.

we understand that every human being is ness. We can safely assume that the peoilently over their broken places, fight of habitual temptation and protect selves.

By grace we do not strike out at people for being weak; instead we wrap our arms around them in their weakness.

The apostle Paul counsels us in our attitude toward weakness: "We who are strong ought to bear with the failings of the weak" (Romans 15:1). The phrase "bear with" is not simply about putting up with someone. It's about lovingly standing with them: "Strength is for service, not status" (Romans 15:2 The Message).

GRACE APPLIED TO SIN

A bandage is designed to be applied to a cut. A contact lens is designed to be applied to vision. Grace is designed, more than anything, to be applied to sin. Even someone else's sin. Even someone else's sin against me.

> Sin . . . doesn't . . . have a chance in competition with the aggressive forgiveness we call grace. When it's sin versus grace, grace wins hands down. . . . Grace . . . invites us into life. (Romans 5:20-21 The Message).

It's ironic that people who follow Christ tend to forget grace and condemn people when we discover they have sinned. We treat offenders as if they should never be given another chance, as if they are no longer deserving of anything good and ought to be rejected—as if sin is somehow in a category beyond the application of grace.

Recently I sat across from two well-known Christian leaders who had each fallen terribly into sin but had confessed and repented, submitting themselves to full church discipline for restoration into community. Both shared stories of people they once considered their friends who would no longer speak with them. One failure, and they had become pariahs. One of the leaders, with authenticity of emotion I will not soon forget, simply thanked me for being willing to be seen with him in public.

German philosopher Friedrich Nietzsche wrote in his autobiography of the ability to "smell" the inmost parts of every soul, especially the "abundant hidden dirt at the bottom" of a character.[10] Such vision, and focus, is our natural tendency; it causes us to rush toward the sin of others with a sense of righteous condemnation and judgment. But we rush too quickly, and in forgetfulness of how the same justice would—and should—be applied to us.

In "The Taming of Smeagol" within Tolkien's *The Lord of the Rings*, Frodo wonders what to do with the despicable Gollum, a loathsome creature who creates pain and difficulties throughout the tale. The memory of a conversation with the wise wizard Gandalf gives Frodo his answer.

What a pity Bilbo did not stab the vile creature, when he had a chance!

Pity? It was pity that stayed his hand. Pity, and Mercy: not to strike without need.

I do not feel any pity for Gollum. He deserves death.

Deserves death! I daresay he does. Many that live deserve death. And some die that deserve life. Can you give that to them? Then be no too eager to deal out death in the name of justice. . . . Even the wise cannot see all ends.[11]

It is for sin that Jesus died to extend grace so that we can love as we are called to love, for as C. S. Lewis once noted, "To be a Christian means to forgive the inexcusable, because God has forgiven the inexcusable in you."[12]

I often find my inward journey to embrace God with my heart, soul, mind and strength effortless in comparison to the arduous climb up the mountain of relational love and grace. Truth be told, there are some people I don't *want* to love. I am so overwhelmed by their differences, weaknesses and sins that I cannot help but dislike, even disdain them.

Every one says forgiveness is a lovely idea, until they have something to forgive.

C. S. LEWIS, *MERE CHRISTIANITY*

But then I look in the mirror.

There are few more defining moments than self-evaluation in the light of truth and in the context of humility. When I look at others with the awareness of my own failings, I see them in the light of grace. And that changes *everything*.

Ten

THE DANGER OF PEOPLE

Hell is other people.
JEAN-PAUL SARTRE

T he Ship Canal Bridge on Interstate 5 in Seattle, Washington—the region's busiest freeway and a primary route for commuters—is a rush-hour nightmare. On August 28, 2001, it was worse than normal. Traffic had come to a complete halt as a twenty-six-year-old woman was preparing to commit suicide.

Tempers flared.

The young woman clung to the side of the bridge, wrestling with the agonies of life that led her to the precipice of the 160-foot drop into Lake Union. Angry motorists, blaming the woman for not choosing a less-traveled site to end her life, exited their cars and began to shout insults at her. The host of a top-rated radio show joined in the assault on the emotionally fragile young woman, airing the sound effect of an object hitting the water.

Police eventually closed the bridge entirely, for the callous taunting of passing motorists, Metro bus passengers and truck drivers was hurting the efforts of the negotiators. This, of course, caused congestions and delays to the north, south and east, which made travelers more angry. More and more people called for the distressed woman to take the plunge, even taking up a profanity-laced chant encouraging her to jump.

She did.[1]

What prompts people armed with cell phones and time, sitting still in traffic with the ability to assist, to respond with such anger and contempt? What leads a heart away from compassion and empathy toward callous indifference—even murderous rage?

It's simple. People are dangerous and cruel. Not can be; *are*.

People have dark sides that are unpredictable and difficult to protect against. They can stab deep into our psyche with utter indifference. And they don't even have to know us. Jon Krakauer tells of two Japanese climbers, accompanied by three Sherpas, who set out for the summit of Mount Everest from the high camp on the northeast ridge. As they made their ascent, they passed a climber, horribly frostbitten but still alive after a night without shelter or oxygen, moaning unintelligibly. Not wanting to put their ascent in jeopardy, they continued climbing. Just beyond the top of the Second Step, they encountered two more climbers in need. No words were passed. No water, food or oxygen exchanged hands. Again, the party moved on, stopping to rest 160 feet away.

One of the Japanese climbers later explained, "We were too tired to help. Above 8,000 meters is not a place where people can afford morality."[2]

But not all expressions of our dark sides are perpetrated on strangers. All too often, we intentionally wound those closest to us. A young boy, overweight and self-conscious, used to sneak into the locker room before his physical education class in order to stretch his T-shirt over his legs so it would not cling to his body. One day, another student stumbled upon him and told everyone he had found the boy trying to hide himself while masturbating. For the rest of the year, wherever the boy went, he was taunted with a nickname suggesting what he had been falsely accused of doing.

Wounds from those close to us are not casual assaults. They drive us to self-protect at all costs. Yet God calls us to love those who wound us in the most vulnerable way imaginable: *as we would ourselves.*

And I, for one, find that hard, because it's not safe.

UNSAFE PEOPLE

Few activities are more fraught with peril than contact with other humans. Safe people can be trusted. They are accepting and supportive. They let us love and be loved. But unsafe people abandon, betray, misunderstand and even attack.

People respond to the hazards of human relationships in different ways.

I have struggled with relational fear and trust, and preferred being alone—not necessarily physically but emotionally. When I became a Christian at the age of twenty, everything about my life changed—not the least of which was my relational world. I was introduced to God's call on my life to be not just with him but with *others* in *deep* community—intimacy, where the masks come off. While my heart longed for such community, I was also terrified. I would have to be *known,* which was torturous for me because it meant being vulnerable—and being vulnerable meant being able to be wounded (and I had been wounded enough) and rejected (and I had been rejected enough).

"I think my father is like the Holy Trinity with three people in him, the one in the morning with the paper, the one at night with the stories and the prayers, and then the one who does the bad thing and comes home with the smell of whiskey and wants us to die for Ireland."

FRANK MCCOURT,
ANGELA'S ASHES

Others struggle with their gravitation *toward* other people. Consider women who visit prisons in order to develop intimate relationships with the inmates. Why would they subject themselves to such men? In the movie *Birdman from Alcatraz,* one inmate finds out. A woman he has corresponded with by mail shows up one day at Alcatraz. He demands to know why she has come all the way from the Midwest to see him.

"Because," she says, "you're the only life I have."[3]

This woman, rather than closing her heart to others, opened it too far, longing so much for human relationships that she would sacrifice her safety and identity to acquire them. She is not alone.

NOT THE FINAL WORD

No one is truly safe in matters of relational connectedness. Some are safer than others, but no one is beyond the wielding of a dagger. The illusion of community is that it actually exists somewhere in a pristine state, if only we could get it right, or find the right one, or find the right set of people to enter into it with.

But the community we long for is not of this world, and no human has been able to extend it to another since the Fall. We are left with tantalizing glimpses that often leave our thirst more parched than quenched. The call to community and love forces us to come to grips with the *reality* of the danger involved. We must settle in our hearts that such realities will not be the final, or defining, word for us on love. We must resist the temptation to self-protect by cutting off all chances of intimacy. As C. S. Lewis noted:

> *"I am afraid to tell you who I am, because if I tell you who I am, you may not like who I am, and it's all that I have."*
>
> JOHN POWELL

> To love at all is to be vulnerable. Love anything, and your heart will certainly be wrung and possibly be broken. If you want to make sure of keeping it intact, you must give your heart to no one, not even to an animal. Wrap it carefully round with hobbies and little luxuries; avoid all entanglements; lock it up safe in the casket or coffin of your

selfishness. But in that casket—safe, dark, motionless, airless—it will change. It will not be broken; it will become unbreakable, impenetrable, irredeemable. . . . The only place outside Heaven where you can be perfectly safe from all the dangers . . . of love is Hell.[4]

It is significant that Joseph, who of all the people represented in the Old Testament exhibited perhaps the most consistent character and most forgiving heart, had to deal the *most* with unsafe people. Joseph was betrayed by his brothers, falsely accused by his employer's wife and abandoned by the man he helped liberate from prison. Yet he named his first son Manasseh ("forget") because "God has made me forget all my trouble" (Genesis 41:51).

RELATIONAL I.Q.

But did he really forget? Doubtful. More likely, he refused to allow his past wounds to speak into his present. Not naively—just intentionally.

Instead Joseph sought to build community. We tend to develop a thin skin and a calloused heart, but Joseph seemed to achieve the opposite: a thick skin and a tender heart. To do what Joseph did, we do not simply shut off our feelings and step into future relationships wearing our innermost feelings on our sleeves. From Joseph we learn to not let our past become the determining factor for all relationships.

From another biblical figure we learn to enter future relationships with openness but also with care. That other character is, surprisingly, Jesus.

> During the time he was in Jerusalem, those days of the Passover Feast, many people noticed the signs he was displaying and, seeing they pointed straight to God, entrusted their lives to him. But Jesus didn't entrust his life to them. He knew them inside and out, knew how untrustworthy they were. He didn't need any help in seeing right through them. (John 2:23-24 The Message)

Jesus was not closed to the risk of intimacy; we know that he was in intimate community with several men and women. But he never approached relationships with reckless abandon. He approached people lovingly, but with a discerning spirit.

Henry Cloud and John Townsend, a pair of Christian clinical psychologists, help us do what Jesus did by helping identify the marks of unsafe people:

- They think they "have it all together" instead of being willing to readily admit their weaknesses.

- They tend to attack and criticize rather than encourage. They often lack grace.

- They have a track record of starting relationships but not finishing them. They look for perfect people, and when someone shows imperfection, they move on.

- They are defensive instead of open to feedback, self-righteous instead of humble.

- They deceive, withhold and manipulate instead of telling the truth.

- They are unstable over time instead of consistent. They go from thing to thing, place to place, person to person.

- They apologize but don't change their behavior.

- They blame others instead of taking responsibility.

- They are more concerned about "me" than "us."

- They resist freedom instead of encouraging it.

- They condemn rather than forgive.

- They gossip rather than keep trust.

- They have a negative influence rather than a positive one.

Safe people are not perfect, but they exhibit a very different set of characteristics.

- They draw us closer to God.

- They draw us closer to others.

- They help us become who God created us to be.

- They dwell with us, connecting in a way that lets us know that they are present.

- They extend grace, giving glimpses of unconditional love and acceptance.

- They are honest and real, living out the truth of God.[5]

People exercising discernment don't look for perfect people or communities but check people's patterns of habitual behavior—safe or unsafe—before increasing the level of intimacy.

HEART-CRY

Is it worth it? Yes.

In spite of the danger, we need people. We need what others bring: comfort, modeling, encouragement and support. Most of all, we need others to bless us with love. As Henri Nouwen suggests:

> To give someone a blessing is the most significant affirmation we can offer. It is more than a word of praise or appreciation; it is more than pointing out someone's talents or good deeds; it is more than putting someone in the light. To give a blessing is to affirm, to say "yes" to a person's Belovedness.[6]

God declared at the dawn of creation that "it is not good for the man to be alone" (Genesis 2:18 NLT). As beings made in the image of God in three persons, we were made to be together. Nouwen received a firsthand lesson on the deep, universal need of community in every life while he was pastor of the mentally handicapped people of Daybreak, a community in Toronto. Shortly before he started a prayer service in one of the houses, Janet, a handicapped member of the community, said, "Henri, can you give me a blessing?" He responded by tracing the sign of the cross on her forehead with his thumb.

She did not feel blessed. "No, that doesn't work. I want a real blessing!"

Nouwen realized that ritual wasn't going to cut it. "Oh, I am sorry," he replied. "Let me give you a real blessing when we are all together for the prayer service."

She nodded with a smile and seemed willing to wait. After the service, when about thirty people were sitting in a circle on the floor, Nouwen still did not know what Janet wanted or what he would do for her. He said, "Janet has asked me for a special blessing. She feels that she needs that now." Janet stood up and walked to where Henri was standing. She put her arms around him and put her head against his chest. He instinctively wrapped his arms around her so that she seemed to vanish in the folds of his robe.

Janet, I want you to know that you are God's Beloved Daughter. You are precious in God's eyes. Your beautiful smile, your kindness to the people in your house and all the good things you do show us what a beautiful human being you are. I know you feel a little low these days and that there is some sadness in your heart, but I want you to remember who you are: a very special person, deeply loved by God and all the people who are here with you.

As he finished, Janet raised her head and looked up into his eyes. Her broad smile told Henri that she had received her blessing. When she returned to her place, a woman raised her hand and said, "I want a blessing too."

She stood up and put her face against his chest as well. He wrapped his arms around her and spoke words of blessing. Many more of the handicapped people followed, expressing the same desire to be blessed in the same way.

The most touching moment for Nouwen came when a twenty-four-year-old student, one of the assistants, raised *his* hand. He laid his head on Nouwen's chest and received his blessing too. Afterward, he looked into Nouwen's face with tears in his eyes and said, "Thank you, thank you very much."[7]

CONCLUSION
Living in Tension

I have come to believe that the highest compliment I can receive as a communicator is "It was like you were speaking right to me" or "It's like you have been reading my diary." Connecting, I have found, has less to do with style than it does with empathy. On the common ground of empathy, one life can flow into another; even better, one life can become open to the Holy Spirit through another.

The irony is that our deepest struggles are the very areas we keep most closed. We never name our greatest challenges, which leads to denial, the most debilitating posture imaginable for spiritual health and growth.

In his book *The Wounded Healer*, Henri Nouwen writes that the main task of the minister is to

prevent people from suffering for the wrong reasons.

Many people suffer because of the false supposition on which they have based their lives. That supposition is that there should be no fear or loneliness, no confusion or doubt.[1]

This sentiment seemed to be behind C. S. Lewis's remark that "if you look for truth, you may find comfort in the end: if you look for comfort you will not get either comfort or truth—only . . . wishful thinking to begin with and, in the end, despair."[2]

The reality of the Christian life is that it is a struggle akin to Jacob's wrestling with God. Jacob did not run from the conflict, for in grappling with God he *seized* God's participation in his life—through wrestling with God he received God's blessing. Struggle with God is the *essence* of relationship with God.

- If there is any tenderness to my heart, it has come through its being broken.

- If anything of worth flows through my soul, it flows out of a desert.

- If there is any trustworthiness to my mind, it was forged on the anvil of doubt.

- If my actions seem vigorous, they originated in blindness and frailty.

- If there is depth to any of my relationships, it has come through wounding.

Not understanding the meaning of the struggles would be devastating; knowing it makes all of the difference in the world. It is how I have embraced this mysterious God who created me. It is why I can move toward loving him with all of my heart, soul, mind and strength. It is why I can extend that love toward his other children.

Not perfectly. Not completely. Just authentically.

NOTES

Introduction

[1]Malcolm Muggeridge, *Confessions of a Twentieth-Century Pilgrim* (San Francisco: Harper & Row, 1988), p. 13.

[2]C. S. Lewis, quoted in David C. Downing, *The Most Reluctant Convert: C. S. Lewis's Journey to Faith* (Downers Grove, Ill.: InterVarsity Press, 2002), p. 12.

[3]M. Scott Peck, *The Different Drum: Community Making and Peace* (New York: Touchstone/Simon & Schuster, 1987), pp. 85-106.

Part One: The Struggle of Our Hearts

[1]Paul Brand and Philip Yancey, *In His Image* (Grand Rapids, Mich.: Zondervan, 1984), p. 58.

Chapter One: The Betrayal of God

[1]Bono, introduction to *Selections from the Book of Psalms* (New York: Grove Press, 1999), p. vii.

[2]Adapted from Lynn Elber, "'West Wing' Ends Season Powerfully," Associated Press, May 17, 2001, as found at <http://dailynews.yahoo.com>; David Bianculli, "In God, They Dis-trust," May 18, 2001, *New York Daily News,* as found at <www.nydailynews.com >; Ted Olsen, "Weblog: TV President: 'To Hell with You, God,'" May 18, 2001, <www.christianitytoday.com>.

[3]As quoted by David Van Biema, "When God Hides His Face," *Time*, July 16, 2001, p. 64.

[4]Søren Kierkegaard, *Philosophical Fragments*, taken from *A Kierkegaard Anthology*, ed. Robert Bretall (Princeton, N.J.: Princeton University Press, 1946), pp. 165-66.

[5]Langdon Gilkey, *Shantung Compound* (San Francisco: HarperSanFrancisco, 1966), pp. 115-16.

[6]As cited by Cornelius Plantinga Jr., *Not the Way It's Supposed to Be* (Grand Rapids, Mich.: Eerdmans, 1995) p. 7.

[7]Philip Yancey, *Where Is God When It Hurts?* (Grand Rapids, Mich.: Zondervan, 1977), pp. 51, 56.

[8]Boethius, *The Consolation of Philosophy*, trans. V. E. Watts (New York: Penguin, 1969), p. 125.

[9]Philip Yancey, *Reaching for the Invisible God* (Grand Rapids, Mich.: Zondervan, 2000), pp. 56-57.

[10]David Van Biema, "When God Hides His Face," *Time*, July 16, 2001, p. 64.

[11]Frederick Buechner, *Wishful Thinking* (New York: Harper & Row, 1973), p. 17.

[12]Os Guinness, *God in the Dark* (Wheaton, Ill.: Crossway, 1996), p. 178.

[13]Bono, *Selections from the Book of Psalms,* p. xii.

Chapter Two: The Exclusivity of God

[1]Belief-O-Matic is powered by <www.SelectSmart.com> and was featured through a link on the America Online homepage that led to <www.beliefnet.com>.

[2]Walter Truett Anderson, *The Truth About the Truth* (New York: Penguin, 1995), p. 6.

[3]As quoted by Toby Lester, "Oh, Gods!" *The Atlantic Monthly* 289, no. 2 (2002): 38.

[4]*Barrett's World Christian Encyclopedia,* 2nd ed. (Oxford: Oxford University Press, 2001).

[5]Malise Ruthven, *The Divine Supermarket: Shopping for God in America* (New York: William Morrow, 1989).

[6] Peter L. Berger, *The Sacred Canopy: Elements of a Sociological Theory of Religion* (Garden City, N.Y.: Doubleday/Anchor, 1969), pp. 127-53.

[7]C. S. Lewis, *Mere Christianity* (New York: Macmillan, 1952), p. 29.

[8]Richard J. Mouw, *He Shines in All That's Fair: Culture and Common Grace* (Grand Rapids, Mich.: Eerdmans, 2001), p. 36.

[9]Ibid., p. 38.

[10]Alan Levine, "The Prehistory of Toleration and Varieties of Skepticism," in

Early Modern Skepticism and the Origins of Toleration, ed. Alan Levine (New York: Lexington, 1999), p. 1.

[11]Allan Bloom, *The Closing of the American Mind* (New York: Simon & Schuster, 1987), pp. 25-26.

[12]The following three distinctions were first suggested to my thinking by John Stott's discussion of religious pluralism in *The Authentic Jesus* (London: Marshall, Morgan & Scott, 1985). See further Harold Netland, *Dissonant Voices: Religious Pluralism and the Question of Truth* (Grand Rapids, Mich.: Eerdmans, 1991), pp. 305-9.

[13]Intellectual tolerance is not to be confused with academic or intellectual freedom, which have their own dynamics and validity.

[14]Ellen Goodman, "Too Much Tolerance Bad for Truth," *The Charlotte Observer,* March 18, 2000, p. 19A.

[15]Adapted from Cliff Knechtle, *Give Me an Answer* (Downers Grove, Ill.: InterVarsity Press, 1986), pp. 28-29.

[16]Richard Rorty, *Contingency, Irony, and Solidarity* (New York: Cambridge University Press, 1989), p. 3.

[17]Will D. Campbell, *Brother to a Dragonfly* (New York: Continuum, 1987), p. 220.

Part Two: The Sturggle of Our Souls

[1]Jean Paul Sartre, *The Devil and the Good Lord,* trans. Kitty Black (New York: Vintage, 1960), pp. 140-41.

Chapter Three: The Distance of God

[1]Martin Marty, *A Cry of Absence* (Grand Rapids Mich.: Eerdmans, 1997), pp. 1-2.

[2]Information taken from several sources, including Laurinda Keys, "Mother Teresa's Spiritual Struggles," *The Charlotte Observer,* September 15, 2001, p. 19A; Satinder Bindra, "Archbishop: Mother Teresa Underwent Exorcism," CNN New Delhi Bureau, September 7, 2001, posted 4:26 p.m. EDT at <www.CNN.com/World>.

[3]Ken Gire, *The Reflective Life* (Colorado Springs: Chariot Victor, 1998), p. 47.

[4]Douglas Steere, *Dimensions of Prayer,* rev. ed. (Nashville: Upper Room, 1997), p. 90.

[5]Philip Yancey, *Reaching for the Invisible God* (Grand Rapids, Mich.: Zondervan, 2000), p. 118.

[6]On this, see Esther de Waal, *Every Earthly Blessing: Rediscovering the Celtic Tradition* (Harrisburg, Penn.: Morehouse, 1999), pp. xv, 1.

[7]Esther de Waal, ed., *The Celtic Vision: Selections from the Carmina Gadelica* (Petersham, Mass.: St. Bede's Publications, 1988), p. 77.

[8]Taken from the wonderful collection of primary sources found in *Celtic Spirituality*, trans. Oliver Davies and Thomas O'Loughlin, Classics of Western Spirituality (New York: Paulist, 1999), p. 120.

[9]Adapted from Roger von Oech, *A Kick in the Seat of the Pants* (San Francisco: Harper Collins, 1986).

Chapter Four: The Silence of God

[1]C. S. Lewis, *A Grief Observed* (San Francisco: Harper & Row, 1961), pp. 7-10.

[2]Ibid., p. 38.

[3]Dallas Willard, *Hearing God* (Downers Grove: InterVarsity Press, 1999), pp. 26-27.

[4]Thomas R. Kelly, *A Testament of Devotion* (New York: Harper & Row, 1941), p. 121.

[5]Anna Muoio, "All the Right Moves," *Fast Company*, May 1999, p. 192.

[6]Kathleen Norris, *Amazing Grace: A Vocabulary of Faith* (New York: Riverhead, 1998), p. 17.

[7]Frederick Buechner, *Whistling in the Dark* (San Francisco: HarperSanFrancisco, 1988), p. 58.

[8]Alan Jones, *Soul Making: The Desert Way of Spirituality* (San Francisco: HarperSanFrancisco, 1985), pp. 6, 62-63.

[9]Larry Crabb, *Shattered Dreams: God's Unexpected Pathway to Joy* (Colorado Springs: WaterBrook, 2001), pp. 158-59.

[10]G. Curtis Jones, "Prayer of an Unknown Confederate Soldier," in *1000 Illustrations* (Nashville: Broadman, 1986), pp. 298-99.

Chapter Five: The Foolishness of God

[1]Richard John Neuhaus, *The Naked Public Square* (Grand Rapids, Mich.: Eerdmans, 1984).

[2]Stephen L. Carter, *The Culture of Disbelief* (New York: BasicBooks, 1993).

[3]Page Smith, *Killing the Spirit: Higher Education in America* (New York: Viking, 1990), p. 5.

[4]J. R. R. Tolkien, *The Fellowship of the Ring*, 2nd ed. (Boston: Houghton Mifflin, 1965), pp. 280-81, 414.

[5]The theory of macroevolution remains highly suspect, failing to account for the actual origin of species. Self-reproducing organisms must be in place for natural selection to even begin. See Michael Behe, *Darwin's Black Box* (New York: Free Press, 1996); Phillip E. Johnson, *Darwin on Trial* (Downers Grove, Ill.: InterVarsity Press, 1991); and William A. Dembski, *Intelligent Design* (Downers Grove, Ill.: InterVarsity Press, 1999).

[6]Freud's argument does not account for many of the intellectual achievements of civilization, including his own theory of psychoanalysis. See Paul Vitz, *Faith of the Fatherless: The Psychology of Atheism* (Dallas: Spence, 1999), p. 6.

[7]See Kathleen Norris, *The Cloister Walk* (New York: Riverhead, 1996), p. 363.

[8]Mark A. Noll, *The Scandal of the Evangelical Mind* (Grand Rapids, Mich.: Eerdmans, 1994), p. 4.

[9]I have explored the most common rational objections to the Christian faith in James Emery White, *A Search for the Spiritual: Exploring Real Christianity* (Grand Rapids, Mich.: Baker, 1998).

[10]Martin Luther, *What Luther Says: An Anthology*, ed. Ewald M. Plass (St. Louis: Concordia, 1959), p. 483.

[11]Os Guinness, *In Two Minds* (Downers Grove, Ill.: InterVarsity Press, 1976), p. 15, 24-25.

[12]Frederick Buechner, *Wishful Thinking* (New York: Harper & Row, 1973), p. 20.

[13]My story is told in detail in White, *Search for the Spiritual*, pp. 14-16.

[14]Correspondence of C. S. Lewis to Sheldon Vanauken in Vanauken's *A Severe Mercy* (New York: Bantam, 1977), p. 133.

[15]Scott Stapp, interviewed by Gavin Edwards, "Sea of Fire," *Spin,* September 2000, p. 111.

[16]Adapted from Humphrey Carpenter, *The Inklings* (New York: Ballantine, 1978), pp. 45-48, as well as my own journeys to Oxford and dialogues with Oxford folk.

Chapter Six: The Mystery of God

[1]David Perlmutt, "Behind the Music, a Passionate Citizen," *The Charlotte Observer*, Sunday, June 10, 2001, p. C1.

[2]Daniel Lanahan, *When God Says No: The Mystery of Suffering and the Dynamics of Prayer* (New York: Lantern, 2001), p. 16.

[3]For a more thorough discussion of paradox see David Basinger, "Biblical Paradox: Does Revelation Challenge Logic?" *Journal of Evangelical Theological Education* 30, no. 2 (1987): 205. See also Scott Burson and Jerry Lo Walls, *C. S. Lewis and Francis Schaeffer* (Downers Grove, Ill.: InterVarsity Press, 1998), pp. 86-87.

[4]C. S. Lewis, *A Grief Observed* (San Francisco: Harper & Row, 1961), p. 55.

[5]Corrie ten Boom, with John and Elizabeth Sherrill, *The Hiding Place* (New York: Bantam, 1974), pp. 26-27.

[6]Kathleen Powers Erickson, *At Eternity's Gate: The Spiritual Vision of Vincent van Gogh* (Grand Rapids, Mich.: Eerdmans, 1998), p. 165, quoting from a letter of van Gogh's written on September 29, 1888.

[7]Rudolf Otto, *The Idea of the Holy*, trans. John W. Harvey (London: Oxford University Press, 1958), p. 31.

[8]Adapted from *The Glenstal Book of Prayer* (Collegeville, Minn.: Liturgical Press, 2001), pp. 98-101.

Chapter Seven: The Will of God

[1]Brennan Manning, *The Ragamuffin Gospel* (Sisters, Ore.: Multnomah Publishers, 1990), p. 22.

[2]M. Blaine Smith, *Knowing God's Will*, 2nd ed. (Downers Grove, Ill.: InterVarsity Press, 1991), pp. 48-49.

[3]Os Guinness, *The Call* (Nashville: Word, 1998), p. 4.

[4]Walter Brueggeman, *Hopeful Imagination*, cited in Kathleen Norris, *Cloister Walk* (New York: Riverhead, 1996), p. 41.

[5]Barbara Tuchman, *The March of Folly* (New York: Alfred A. Knopf, 1984).

Chapter Eight: The Deception of God

[1]Adapted from Melody Petersen, "A Résumé Distinguished by What It Didn't Mention," *The New York Times on the Web*, September 6, 2001, <www.nytimes.com>.

²Kathleen Norris, *The Cloister Walk* (New York: Riverhead, 1996), p. 45.

³Larry Crabb, *Shattered Dreams* (Colorado Springs: WaterBrook, 2001), pp. 30-32.

⁴David Ireland with Louis Tharp Jr., *Letters to an Unborn Child* (New York: Harper & Row, 1974), pp. 117-18.

⁵Nancy Guthrie, as cited by David Van Biema, "When God Hides His Face," *Time*, July 16, 2001.

⁶Jim Collins, *Good to Great* (New York: HarperBusiness, 2001), pp. 83-85.

⁷C. S. Lewis, *The Last Battle* (New York: HarperTrophy, 1994), pp. 210-11.

Chapter Nine: The Dislike of People

¹Adapted from Mark Price, ":(You've got bad breath :(" *The Charlotte Observer*, August 15, 2001, p. 1A.

²Kathleen Norris, *The Cloister Walk* (New York: Riverhead, 1996), p. 21.

³Alexa Albert, *Brothel: Mustang Ranch and Its Women* (New York: Random House, 2001), p. 234.

⁴Larry Crabb, *Connecting* (Nashville: Word, 1997), pp. 13, 15.

⁵Mother Teresa, cited by Philip Yancey, *The Jesus I Never Knew* (Grand Rapids, Mich.: Zondervan, 1995), p. 233.

⁶C. S. Lewis, *The Weight of Glory* (New York: Macmillan/Collier, 1949), p. 19.

⁷Adapted from Christopher de Vinck, *The Power of the Powerless* (Grand Rapids, Mich.: Zondervan, 1988), pp. 27-33.

⁸Mother Teresa, interviewed by Malcolm Muggeridge, *Something Beautiful for God: Mother Teresa of Calcutta* (San Francisco: Harper & Row, 1971), p. 113.

⁹C. S. Lewis, *Mere Christianity* (New York: Macmillan, 1943), p. 101.

¹⁰As cited by Philip Yancey, *What's So Amazing About Grace* (Grand Rapids: Zondervan, 1997), p. 280.

¹¹J. R. R. Tolkien, *The Lord of the Rings: The Two Towers,* 2nd ed. (Boston: Houghton Mifflin, 1965), p. 221. Italics in original.

¹²C. S. Lewis, "On Forgiveness," in *The Weight of Glory and Other Addresses* (New York: Collier/Macmillan, 1980), p. 125.

Chapter Ten: The Danger of People

¹Adapted from Gordy Holt, "High-Profile Suicide Attempt Draws Nation's Attention," *Seattle Post-Intelligencer*, August 30, 2001; Robert L. Jamieson Jr.,

"Exploiting Woman's Plight for Ratings," *Seattle Post-Intelligencer*, August 30, 2001; and Candy Hatcher, "Woman's Plight Brought Out Worst in Many," *Seattle Post-Intelligencer*, August 29, 2001; posted on <www.MSNBC.com> August 30, 2001.

[2]Jon Krakauer, *Into Thin Air: A Personal Account of the Mt. Everest Disaster* (New York: Villard, 1997), pp. 240-41.

[3]Adapted from Ted Conover, *Newjack: Guarding Sing Sing* (New York: Random House, 2000), p. 156.

[4]C. S. Lewis, *The Four Loves* (New York: Harvest/Harcourt Brace Jovanovich, 1960), p. 169.

[5]Henry Cloud and John Townsend, *Safe People* (Grand Rapids, Mich.: Zondervan, 1995), pp. 28-39, 143, 145-46.

[6]Henri Nouwen, *Life of the Beloved* (New York: Crossroad, 1993), p. 56.

[7]Adapted from ibid., pp. 57-59.

Conclusion

[1]Henri Nouwen, *The Wounded Healer* (Garden City, N.Y.: Image, 1979), p. 93.

[2]C. S. Lewis, *Mere Christianity* (New York: Macmillan, 1943), p. 25.